Better Homes and Gar[dens]

COUNTRY DOLLS

/ 5 4 9 6 5 /

745,592
B466

WE CARE!

The Crafts Department at Better Homes and Gardens® Books assembled this collection of
projects for your crafting pleasure. Our staff is committed to providing you with clear
and concise instructions so that you can complete each project. We guarantee your satisfaction
with this book for as long as you own it. We welcome your comments and suggestions.
Please address your correspondence to Better Homes and Gardens® Book Crafts Department,
1716 Locust Street, LS-352X, Des Moines, IA 50336.

© Copyright 1991 by Meredith Corporation, Des Moines, Iowa.
All Rights Reserved. Printed in the United States of America.
First Edition. Printing Number and Year: 5 4 3   96 95 94 93 92
Library of Congress Catalog Card Number: 90-64101
ISBN: 0-696-01915-9 (hard cover)
ISBN: 0-696-01916-7 (trade paperback)

BETTER HOMES AND GARDENS® BOOKS

Vice President, Editorial Director: Elizabeth P. Rice
Art Director: Ernest Shelton
Managing Editor: David A. Kirchner
Project Editors: James D. Blume, Marsha Jahns
Project Managers: Liz Anderson,
  Jennifer Speer Ramundt, Angela K. Renkoski

Crafts Editor: Sara Jane Treinen
Senior Crafts Editors: Beverly Rivers,
  Patricia Wilens
Associate Crafts Editor: Nancy Reames

Associate Art Directors: Neoma Thomas,
  Linda Ford Vermie, Randall Yontz
Assistant Art Directors: Lynda Haupert,
  Harijs Priekulis, Tom Wegner
Graphic Designers: Mary Schlueter Bendgen,
  Michael Burns, Mick Schnepf
Art Production: Director, John Berg;
  Associate, Joe Heuer;
  Office Manager, Michaela Lester

President, Book Group: James F. Stack
Vice President, Retail Marketing: Jamie L. Martin
Vice President, Administrative Services: Rick Rundall

BETTER HOMES AND GARDENS® MAGAZINE
President, Magazine Group: James A. Autry
Editorial Director: Doris Eby

MEREDITH CORPORATION OFFICERS
Chairman of the Executive Committee: E. T. Meredith III
Chairman of the Board: Robert A. Burnett
President and Chief Executive Officer: Jack D. Rehm

COUNTRY DOLLS
Editor: Beverly Rivers
Graphic Designer: Harijs Priekulis
Project Manager: Jennifer Speer Ramundt
Contributing Writer: Sharon L. Novotne O'Keefe
Contributing Illustrator: Chris Neubauer
Electronic Text Processor: Paula Forest

Cover projects: See page 4.

CONTENTS

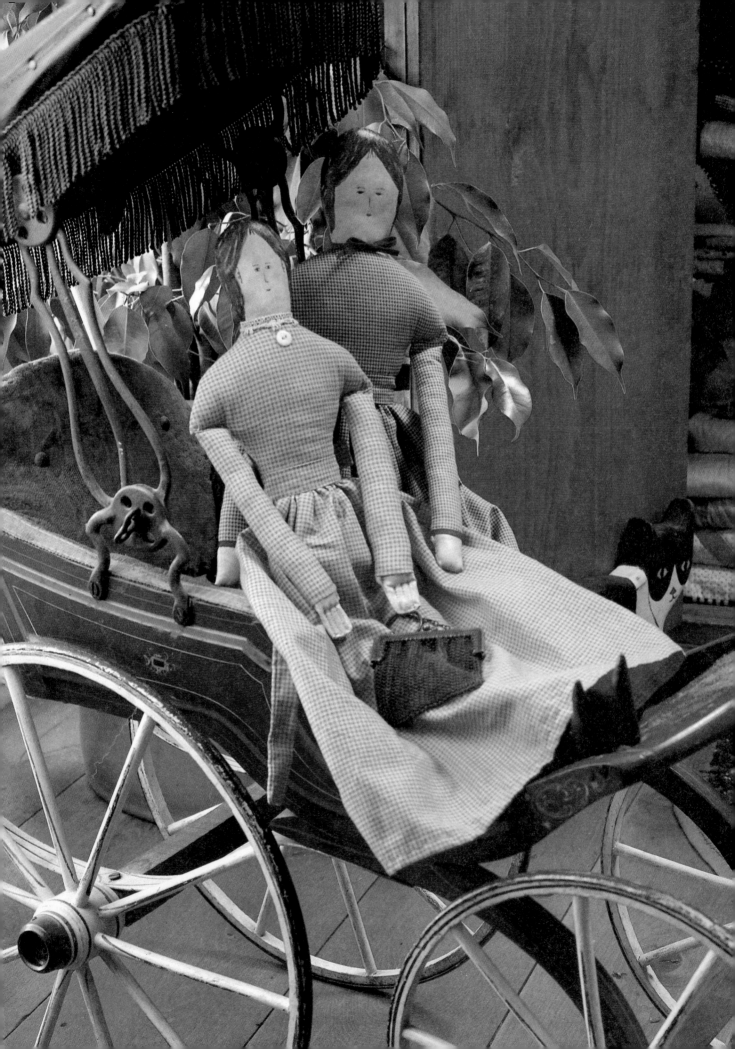

HEIRLOOM DOLLS

♦ ♦ ♦

Fond memories of treasure hunts in Grandma's attic inspired the collection of old-fashioned muslin dolls in this chapter. Like beloved antiques, these folk art designs will become the heirlooms of tomorrow. Snippets of fabric and floss and quick strokes of paint give each of these handcrafted dolls individuality.

Ducks and geese better scurry. Amy and her little sister, Andrea, *left*, are settled in the surrey, waiting for cousin Abigail to join them for a ride in the country.

The dolls are alike except for size. By sharing the same pattern and a variety of fabric scraps, the dolls can be made to look the same or totally different.

The dolls' bodies and legs are stitched from calicoes and checks. Stuffed with polyester fiberfill, these pieces become their blouses and leggings. Only the skirts and waistbands are added, along with buttons, lace, and other trims.

Faces, hands, shoes, and socks are painted onto muslin with acrylic paints. The muslin then is antiqued and varnished to make the dolls resemble those that Grandmother might have played with.

Ranging in size from 18½ to 24 inches, these dolls can be stitched from the full-size patterns that begin on page 10.

everly Sue, *opposite,* anxiously anticipates the arrival of her beau. Quite certain that this will be the day he pops the big question, she is wearing her finest floral dress, which is embellished with bits of old lace.

Jeffrey, *above,* is trying to be patient, but his train has been delayed. Wearing his best trousers and a splashy red tie, he has his hopes high that he may be able to whisk Beverly Sue off to the big city.

Both dolls are constructed from the same pattern. Arms and legs are buttoned on.

Stitching across the knees and elbows makes the muslin bodies flexible for sitting or standing.

Use the facial features on page 15, or adjust them to resemble family or friends. A single strand of embroidery floss for eyes, nose, and mouth, and a bit of powder blush on the cheeks makes these dolls quite realistic.

Braided wool is unraveled for Beverly Sue's long curls and Jeffrey's graying locks.

A source for ordering curly wool is included with the instructions that begin on page 12.

Angelica, *left,* is determined to bless all creatures great and small. She's starting with a wagon full of tiny teddy bears.

This charming angel is proof that the most simple construction can produce ingenious results.

Tea-dyed fabrics and an old worn quilt scrap give this celestial beauty true country appeal. Her endearing gaze is dotted on with a permanent marker and a dash of powder blush. Golden flax is stitched in place for hair, and a wreath of evergreen and dried flowers adorns her crown.

A fabric star at the tip of a small twig sprinkles stardust on all her surroundings.

Perfect for a centerpiece or treetop, or just tucked inside an old pine cupboard, this 15-inch angel will be hard to part with. But, because she's easy to make, you can craft a host of them in a jiffy.

Instructions begin on page 16.

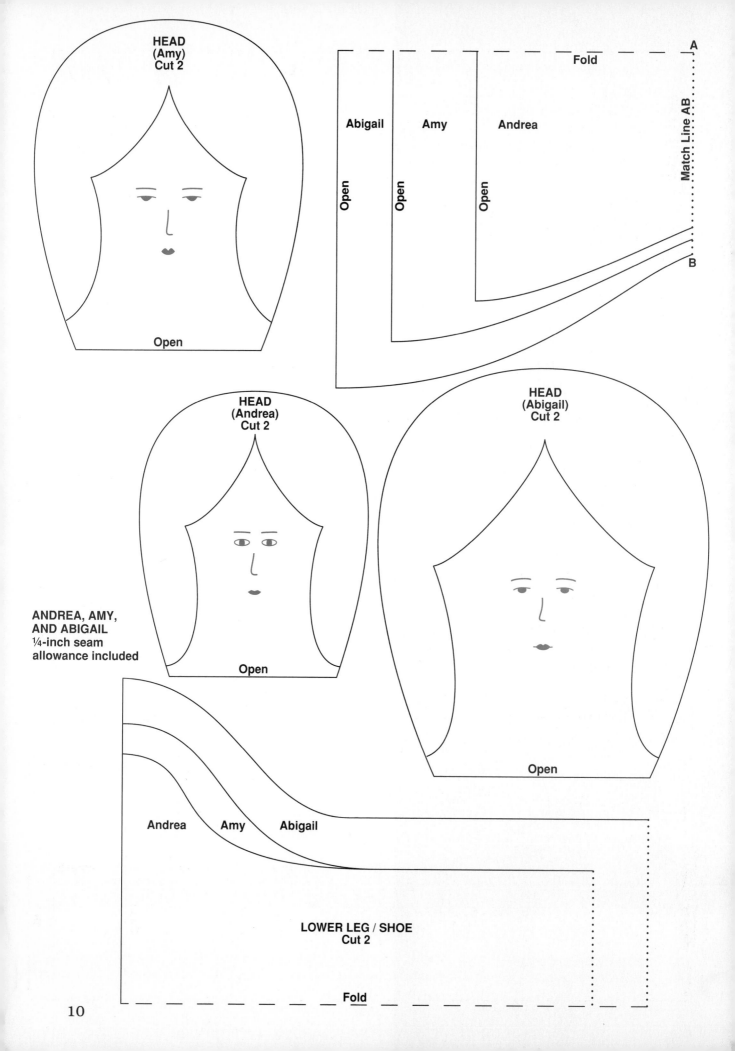

HEAD
(Amy)
Cut 2

Open

Fold   A

Abigail   Amy   Andrea

Open   Open   Open

Match Line AB

B

HEAD
(Andrea)
Cut 2

Open

HEAD
(Abigail)
Cut 2

Open

ANDREA, AMY,
AND ABIGAIL
¼-inch seam
allowance included

Andrea   Amy   Abigail

LOWER LEG / SHOE
Cut 2

Fold

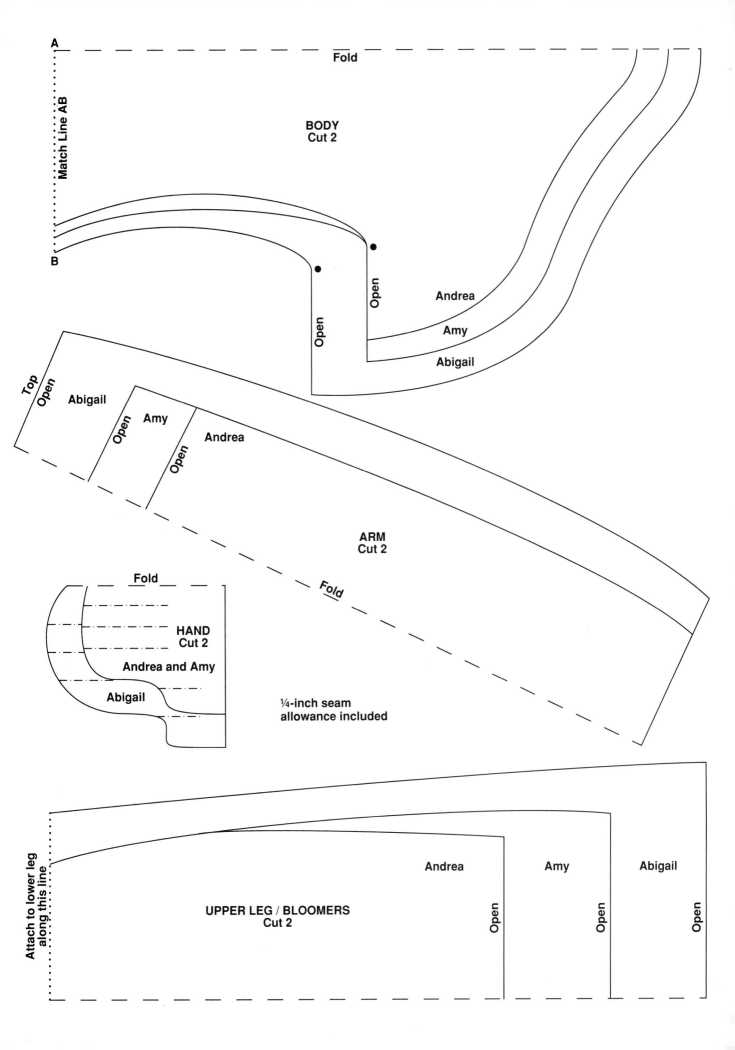

Andrea, Amy, and Abigail

Shown on pages 4 and 5.

Finished height of each doll is as follows: 18½ inches (Andrea, page 4, *left*), 21½ inches (Amy, page 4, *right*), 24 inches (Abigail, page 5).

MATERIALS
For one doll
1¼ yards of homespun cotton checked fabric
½ yard of muslin
¼ yard of calico print for bloomers
Scraps of lace
Button (optional)
Ribbon (optional)
Tea bags (for staining)
Polyester fiberfill
Acrylic paint in off-white, black, brown, and red
Satin-finish clear varnish
Pine-color wood stain
Knitting needle or other blunt-pointed object
Tracing paper

INSTRUCTIONS
A ¼-inch seam allowance is included with each pattern. Use ¼-inch seams on all stitching.

Solid lines on pattern pieces are cutting lines; broken lines indicate where a pattern piece is placed on the fabric fold for cutting. Lines that alternate dots and dashes indicate topstitching. Blue lines on head patterns are guides for painting faces.

Trace patterns on pages 10 and 11 onto tracing paper. Cut out paper patterns. For the body, align the AB markings on the body piece on page 10 with the AB markings on the body piece on page 11 to make one pattern.

Tea-dye muslin, check, and print fabrics before cutting. To tea-dye, boil 4 cups of water with eight tea bags. Remove bags; soak all fabrics in the tea. Remove fabrics and let them dry thoroughly.

From muslin, cut head, hands, and lower leg/shoe pieces. From check, cut arms, body, and a skirt rectangle as follows: 25x16½ inches (Abigail), 24x15 inches (Amy), or 24x12 inches (Andrea).

Also from check, cut waist sash as follows: 19½x2¼ inches (Abigail), 19x1¾ inches (Amy), or 18½x1¾ inches (Andrea). From print, cut upper leg/bloomers.

To assemble the body
With right sides together, stitch around head pieces, leaving neck open. Clip curves; turn right side out and press.

Fold bottom edge of one upper leg/bloomer piece under ¼ inch; press. Lay folded edge of upper leg over top edge of lower leg/shoe piece; topstitch the two pieces together. With right sides together, fold leg in half and stitch. Leave top open for turning. Trim seams; clip curves and turn. Use a blunt-pointed object such as a knitting needle to push toes of shoes out. Stuff the shoe and leg. Repeat for the second leg; set legs aside.

Turn ¼ inch under on bottom (wrist) of arm piece; press. Position arm over the top of hand piece; topstitch. With right sides together, fold arm in half. Stitch seams, leaving top edge (shoulder) open. Trim seams; clip curves and turn.

The larger and smaller dolls have topstitching on the hands to define fingers. (See marks on pattern on page 11.) To sew fingers, put a small amount of fiberfill in hand and topstitch following the pattern markings.

Finish stuffing both arms.

Stitch body around the top and down the sides, leaving open the armhole areas and the bottom.

Turn armhole openings on body in ¼ inch and insert the arms approximately 1 inch into body. Topstitch across the armhole openings through all layers.

Firmly stuff the body. Stuff the head. Turn ¼ inch of the fabric at the bottom of the head piece (neck) to the inside. Set the head on top of the neck area of the body and hand-stitch the head to body.

Fold ¼ inch of the bottom edge of body to the inside; press. With toes pointing forward and the leg seam running down the front of each leg, insert legs into the bottom opening on the body. Topstitch across the bottom of the body through all layers.

Painting the doll
Paint the head, hands, and legs with off-white acrylic paint. Let dry. Repeat. Paint boots black (shaded area on lower leg/shoe pattern indicates where to paint for boot). Paint hair, nose, and eyes brown, and mouth red, using the head pattern as a guide for positioning the features. Paint the back of the head brown. Let dry. Brush stain over all painted areas. Wipe off excess stain with a rag; dry thoroughly. Brush on varnish. Let dry. *Note:* If varnish is applied over wet stain, a milky filmy appearance will result.

Making the skirt
With right sides facing, stitch short sides of skirt rectangle together. Turn hem under ⅝ inch and stitch. Sew gathering stitches to skirt top. Gather skirt to fit doll's waist; hand-stitch in place at doll's waist.

Fold right sides of waist sash together. Stitch, leaving a 2-inch opening at the center of one long side. Trim corners. Turn right side out; press. Stitch opening closed. Place over gathering on skirt and tie in a bow in back.

Optional: Tack lace to bottom of bloomers and around doll's neck. Sew button at dress front.

Beverly Sue and Jeffrey

Shown on pages 6 and 7.

Finished height of each doll is 18½ inches.

MATERIALS
For one doll
½ yard of muslin for body
Scraps of dark brown, light brown, rose, and salmon embroidery floss
Wool or synthetic hair
Four ¾-inch-diameter buttons for joining arms and legs to body
Polyester fiberfill
Fusible interfacing
Tracing paper
5x10-inch piece of ecru knit for stockings
¼-inch-wide elastic
Purchased shoes

For Beverly Sue's clothing
½ yard of floral print for dress
⅓ yard of muslin for pantaloons
Three ¼-inch buttons or snaps
    for dress
Eyelet and ribbon trims

For Jeffrey's clothing
⅓ yard of navy tweed for slacks
⅓ yard of cotton print for shirt
Four small buttons for shirt
Grosgrain ribbon for suspenders
Two small buttons for
    suspenders

INSTRUCTIONS
Trace the patterns on pages 14–16 onto tracing paper. Add ¼-inch seam allowances to all pieces before cutting. Use ¼-inch seams on all stitching.

Solid lines on patterns are cutting lines; broken lines indicate where a pattern piece is placed on the fabric fold for cutting. Lines that alternate dots and dashes indicate a stitch line (darts, special topstitching). Embroidery stitch outlines appear in blue.

Transfer the head front onto muslin fabric. Trace facial features onto the head front. Do not cut out head front until the face is embroidered.

To embroider the face
Use two strands of rose floss and satin stitches to work the woman's mouth; use salmon floss for the man's mouth. Use two strands of brown floss and satin stitches for eyes. Use two strands of brown and the outline stitch for the eyebrows and nose. Alternate brown and dark brown long stitches for the mustache. Add a dark brown French knot in the center of each of the man's eyes.

Cut out head front piece; press.

To make the body
Cut the body, leg, arm, and head back pieces from muslin fabric.

LEGS: To reinforce buttonholes, fuse strips of interfacing to the wrong sides of buttonhole markings. With right sides facing, sew legs together in sets, leaving an opening between the dots marked on the pattern.

Clip curves and turn legs to the right side. Topstitch along the dot/dash line at the top of each leg. Make ¾-inch buttonholes at the top of each leg. Stuff the upper legs firmly with fiberfill to the second stitching line. On each leg, with foot pointing upward and front and back leg seams together, stitch across knee line as shown on pattern. Stuff lower legs and feet. Hand-stitch the openings closed. Set aside.

ARMS: Follow directions, *above,* for assembling legs.

HEAD: With right sides facing, sew front and back of head together, leaving neck open. Clip curves, and turn right side out. Stuff firmly; set aside.

BODY: With right sides facing, sew front to back, leaving open the neck (between dots) and across the bottom. Sew along V-shaped dot-and-dash line at bottom opening as marked on the pattern. Sew twice to reinforce. Cut down center of V from bottom to point.

Fold body so inner leg seam line and outer seam line of one side match. Stitch across bottom opening. Repeat for other side.

To square the shoulders, fold upper body so shoulder seam line and outer body seam line meet and shoulder forms a triangle. Mark straight line across triangle, ¼ inch from point; stitch on line. Repeat for other shoulder.

Turn body right side out; stuff firmly. Turn neck opening ¼ inch to the inside. Slide neck into neck opening, matching side seams. Slip-stitch head to body.

Mark position on body for arm buttons by aligning top of arm with shoulder. Mark position for leg buttons by placing doll in sitting position so backs of legs are even with base of doll. Sew buttons at marks; button the arms and legs to the doll.

HAIR: The hair used on the dolls on pages 6 and 7 is 100 percent wool from All Cooped Up, 560 S. State, No. B1, Orem, UT 84058. Or, you may use mohair instead.

Glue or hand-stitch the hair in place on the doll's head in the desired hairstyle. Trim to shape.

To make Beverly Sue's clothes
From floral fabric, cut bodice front and back and bodice front and back facings, following the cutting line for the dress. Cut pantaloons, following the fold for pantaloons, from muslin.

DRESS: Sew bodice front to back pieces at shoulder seams. Repeat for facing. Baste pregathered ecru trim to bodice neckline for collar.

With right sides together, sew bodice to facing along neckline and back opening. Turn and press. With wrong sides together, baste bodice to facing along side and waistline.

Open bodice flat. With right sides facing, center and sew sleeve to shoulder, matching dot at bodice shoulder seam to dot on sleeve shoulder seam. Repeat with second sleeve. Sew underarm and side seams. Hem sleeves.

Lap left side of back over right by ½ inch and baste together at waistline.

From floral fabric, cut a 10½x28-inch rectangle for skirt. Fold fabric in half widthwise so it measures 10½x14. At the top raw edge of the folded fabric, measure in 7½ inches from the folded edge and mark the fabric with a dot. Measure down from the top along the fold line 1¼ inches and make a second mark. Connect dots with straight line. Cut on the line, removing a triangular-shaped piece of fabric. (This fabric is cut away so that you can easily gather the skirt to fit the V-shaped waistline on the bodice.)

Sew short ends together for center back seam. Make two tucks along the bottom of the skirt, referring to the photograph on page 6. Hem the skirt.

Sew two rows of gathering threads along the skirt waistline; pull gathers to fit bodice. Sew skirt to bodice at waistline, matching V-shaped center front. Sew small buttons and buttonholes or snaps at back opening.

PANTALOONS: Hem legs; trim with pregathered ecru edging.

With right sides facing, sew pieces together along the center front/back seam. Turn under ½ inch twice along waistline to form
continued

the casing; sew, leaving an opening to insert elastic. Cut elastic to fit doll's waist comfortably; insert the elastic through casing and secure ends with thread.

Cut two 4-inch pieces of elastic. Sew the elastic ⅜ inch from hemmed edge of pantaloons, stretching elastic as you sew to create gathers. Trim excess. Repeat for other leg. Sew inner leg seams.

To make Jeffrey's clothing
Cut the man's shirt from cotton print fabric. Cut one 3x6-inch rectangle from print for the shirt collar. Cut two tie pieces from contrasting print. Cut the slacks from navy tweed.

SHIRT: The shirt pattern is the same as the bodice for the woman's dress, except that the front becomes the back, and the back becomes the front. Also, be sure to use the cutting line for the shirt.

Sew back to front at shoulder seams. Repeat for facing.

With right sides facing, fold collar rectangle in half widthwise. Stitch across short ends. Turn collar fabric right side out. With right side of collar to wrong side of shirt neckline, baste collar to shirt.

Sew shirt to shirt facing along neckline and front edges, taking care not to catch collar in seams. Trim seams; clip curves. Turn and press. With wrong sides together, baste shirt to facing at side and waistline seams.

Sew sleeve to shoulder, matching dots at the shoulder; repeat with second sleeve. Sew underarm and side seams. Repeat for other side. Narrowly hem sleeves.

Place shirt on doll. Lap left side of front over right and sew small buttons down the front through both layers. Fold collar completely upward over the chin.

TIE: With right sides facing, sew tie pieces together. Leave top open. Trim seams; turn right side out and press. Form a knot with the top of the tie. Tack in place at the neckline of the shirt. Turn half of the collar down and tack it in place on each side of the tie.

continued

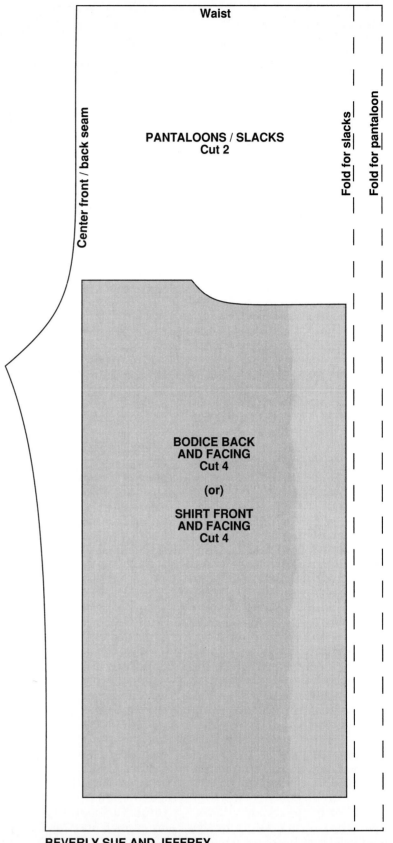

BEVERLY SUE AND JEFFREY
Add ¼-inch seam allowance

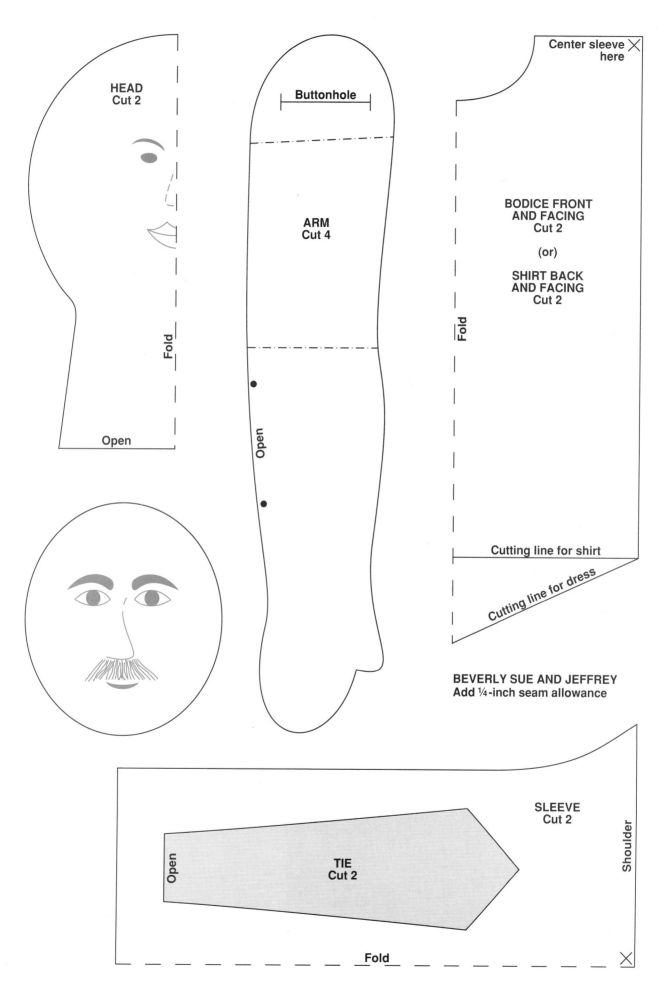

HEAD
Cut 2

Fold

Open

Buttonhole

ARM
Cut 4

Open

Center sleeve here

BODICE FRONT AND FACING
Cut 2

(or)

SHIRT BACK AND FACING
Cut 2

Fold

Cutting line for shirt

Cutting line for dress

BEVERLY SUE AND JEFFREY
Add ¼-inch seam allowance

SLEEVE
Cut 2

Shoulder

Open

TIE
Cut 2

Fold

15

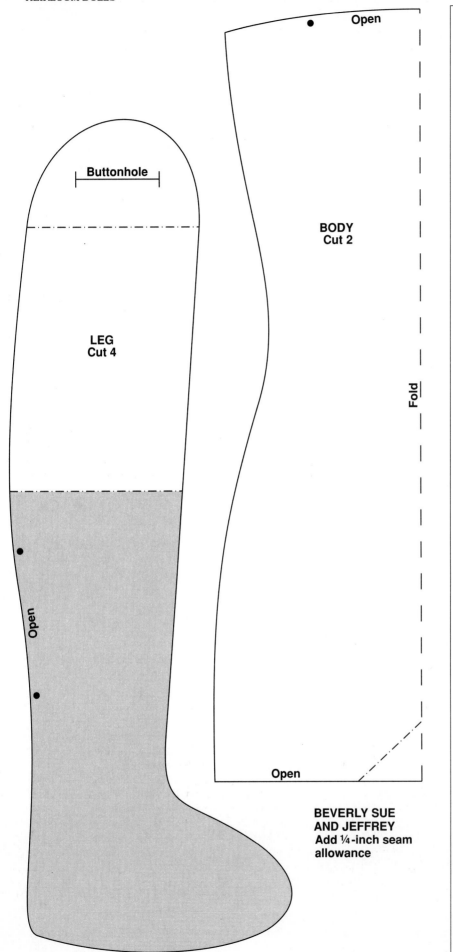

Buttonhole

**LEG
Cut 4**

Open

Open

**BODY
Cut 2**

Fold

Open

**BEVERLY SUE
AND JEFFREY
Add ¼-inch seam
allowance**

SLACKS: The pantaloon/slacks pattern is on page 14. Place the pattern on the fabric fold along the line designated for slacks; cut slacks from navy tweed.

Hem legs. With right sides facing, sew pieces together along center front/back seam. Turn under ½ inch twice along waistline to form the casing; sew, leaving an opening to insert elastic. Cut elastic to fit doll's waist; insert through casing and secure.

Use slacks fabric or grosgrain ribbon for suspenders. Sew buttons in place where suspenders fasten to slacks.

To make stockings for both dolls
Use the shaded portion of the leg pattern to make stockings. Cut four stocking pieces from knit fabric for each doll. Sew pieces together in pairs, leaving top edge open. Turn right side out.

To order shoes for dolls
Shoes can be purchased from your local doll supply shop or from Jo's Dolls, 111 Army Post Road, Des Moines, IA 50315. Beverly Sue's beige shoes with rosettes are Size 40mm. Jeffrey's black boots are Size 65mm.

Angelica

Shown on page 8.

Finished height of doll is 15 inches.

MATERIALS
20 tea bags
⅓ yard of muslin for body
 and wing backs
½ yard of 45-inch-wide batiste
 for dress sleeves and bodice,
 underskirt, and bloomers
½ yard of homespun or cotton
 fabric for apron
Tan buttonhole twist thread
Threads to match fabric
Brown fine-tipped fabric marker
Light pink powdered rouge
Brown acrylic paint
Tracing paper
Polyester fiberfill
1 yard of ¼-inch-wide ribbon
Scrap of fusible webbing
10x14 inches of batting

Scrap of cotton or old quilt
for wing fronts
Twig for wand
Mohair or flax for hair
Crafts glue
Small pieces of dried evergreens
and dried flowers for the halo

INSTRUCTIONS

Trace patterns on pages 18 and 19 onto tracing paper. Add a ¼-inch seam allowance to all pattern pieces before cutting. Use ¼-inch seams on all stitching.

Solid lines on pattern are cutting lines; broken lines indicate where a pattern is placed on the fabric fold for cutting. Lines that alternate dots and dashes indicate stitch lines (darts, special topstitching). A guide for painted features appears in blue.

To tea-dye the fabric

In a large pot, brew 20 tea bags. Remove bags. Place muslin and batiste fabrics in tea and let them set until fabrics are the color you want. Rinse fabrics in cold water; dry thoroughly.

To assemble the body

Cut body, arms, legs, and head from tea-dyed muslin.

With right sides facing, sew together body pieces and leg pieces. Leave openings as marked on the patterns. Clip curves; turn.

With right sides facing, sew head back pieces together along back center line, leaving an opening between the dots. Clip curves.

With right sides facing, sew head back to head front, matching center points at top and bottom. Clip curves; turn. Stuff the head firmly and stitch the opening closed. Set the head aside.

Stuff legs firmly to the stitching line. With seam lines together and toe facing forward, sew each leg across the stitching line. Do not stuff top of leg. Turn bottom of body under ¼ inch; press.

Position legs inside body front at X markings on pattern; baste legs to body front.

Stuff body and hand-stitch bottom closed, encasing legs.

Place a small amount of stuffing in the hand. Hand- or machine-stitch the finger lines shown on pattern on page 18.

Stuff each arm to the stitching line; stitch across arm. Stuff remainder of arm. Slip-stitch the opening closed.

With thumb facing to the front, stitch the arm to the shoulder. Repeat with the other arm.

To paint the face

Dab rouge onto the doll's cheeks. With a fine-tipped fabric marker, draw the eyes and nose following the pattern on page 18.

To make the clothes

SHOES: The shaded area on the leg pattern piece on page 19 is the shoe. Paint the shoes with brown acrylic paint; allow paint to dry. Beginning at the top of the shoe, and leaving a 6-inch tail, use the buttonhole twist to make cross-stitch shoe laces. Make the first half of the stitch going down the shoe and the second half of the stitch going back up the shoe. Leave a 6-inch tail at the end. Tie into a bow.

BLOOMERS: Cut bloomers from batiste fabric. With right sides together, stitch curved seam. Turn under a ¼-inch hem on the bottom of each leg; hem.

With right sides facing, stitch the inside of the legs. Turn bloomers right side out. (If bloomers are loose, take a small tuck to tighten.)

UNDERSKIRT: Cut a 9x45-inch strip of batiste fabric for the underskirt. Cut a 7x2-inch strip for the waistband.

Turn one long side of the skirt fabric under ¼ inch; hem.

With right sides facing, sew two short ends together, leaving a 3-inch opening at the top. Press raw edges of opening to the inside.

With right sides facing, fold the waistband in half lenthwise and stitch across the short ends; turn and press. Turn edges of waistband under ¼ inch; press.

Gather the waist of the underskirt to fit the waistband. Topstitch the waistband in place over the top of the gathered skirt.

Place the underskirt on the angel and whipstitch the waistband closed at the back.

DRESS: Cut the dress bodice from tea-dyed homespun or cotton fabric. Cut yoke pieces from batiste.

For the skirt, cut a 10-inch piece of homespun or cotton the full width of the fabric. Cut two 5x10-inch rectangles from batiste for the sleeves.

Open the dress bodice and lay it flat. Machine-appliqué the two layers of yoke to front of the bodice. See bodice pattern on page 19 for positioning.

Turn one long side of the sleeve under ¼ inch and stitch. Gather the opposite side to fit the armhole opening of the bodice. With right sides facing, sew sleeve in place. Repeat for second sleeve.

Cut skirt fabric in half lengthwise. Press one long side of each piece of skirt fabric under ¼ inch twice and stitch. Gather the unfinished long edges of each piece. With right sides facing, attach half of the skirt to the bodice front and the other half to the bodice back.

With right sides facing, sew the underarm of the sleeve and down the sides of the skirt. Turn the dress to the right side. Press.

Cut the dress collar from batiste fabric. Sew a ¼-inch seam around the collar pieces, leaving an opening for turning. Trim seams; clip curves. Turn and press. Top-stitch around all edges.

Place the dress on the doll and tack in place at the neckline. Place the collar around the neck and tack in place. Add a small bow at the front.

Hand-gather the sleeves at the wrists; knot the ends to secure.

Hand-sew doll's head to body, aligning the X on the body pattern with the bottom of the nose.

continued

To make the wings

Use a piece of a tattered antique quilt, piece a new square, or use homespun or cotton fabric that coordinates with the angel's dress to make wings.

Cut wing pieces from fabrics as listed on the pattern. Do not add the ¼-inch seam allowance to batting piece. Baste batting wings to wrong side of wing fronts. With right sides facing, sew fronts to backs in sets, leaving an opening for turning; turn. Slip-stitch openings closed.

Whipstitch wings together at center back as marked on the pattern. Tack in place at the center back of the angel's head and secure with additional tacking along the back of the dress.

To make the wand

Following manufacturer's instructions, fuse two 2x2-inch pieces of muslin together. Cut the star from fused muslin. Glue a 4-inch piece of twig to the back of the star. Glue the other end of the twig to the angel's hand, wrapping her fingers around the twig.

To make the hair and halo

The doll hair pictured on page 8 is natural flax and can be purchased from a weaving supply store. Mohair can be substituted.

Cut 8-inch lengths of flax or mohair, and lay them flat to a width of 1¾ inches. Machine-stitch a hair part through the middle of the lengths. Cut 1-inch pieces and glue in place for bangs. Glue the hair in place, centering the part on top of the head.

Make a halo from small pieces of dried evergreens. Attach the halo to the top of the head. Add dried flowers, if desired.

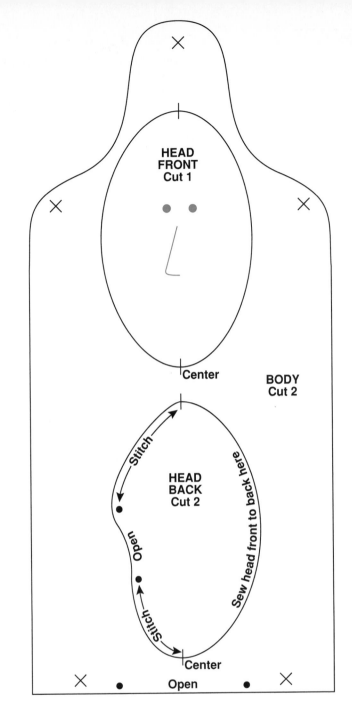

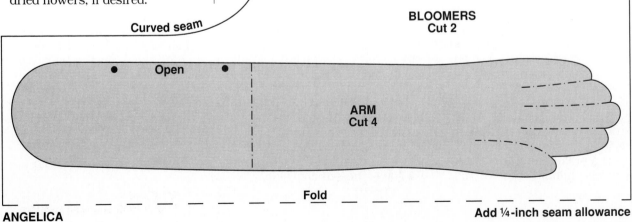

ANGELICA

Add ¼-inch seam allowance

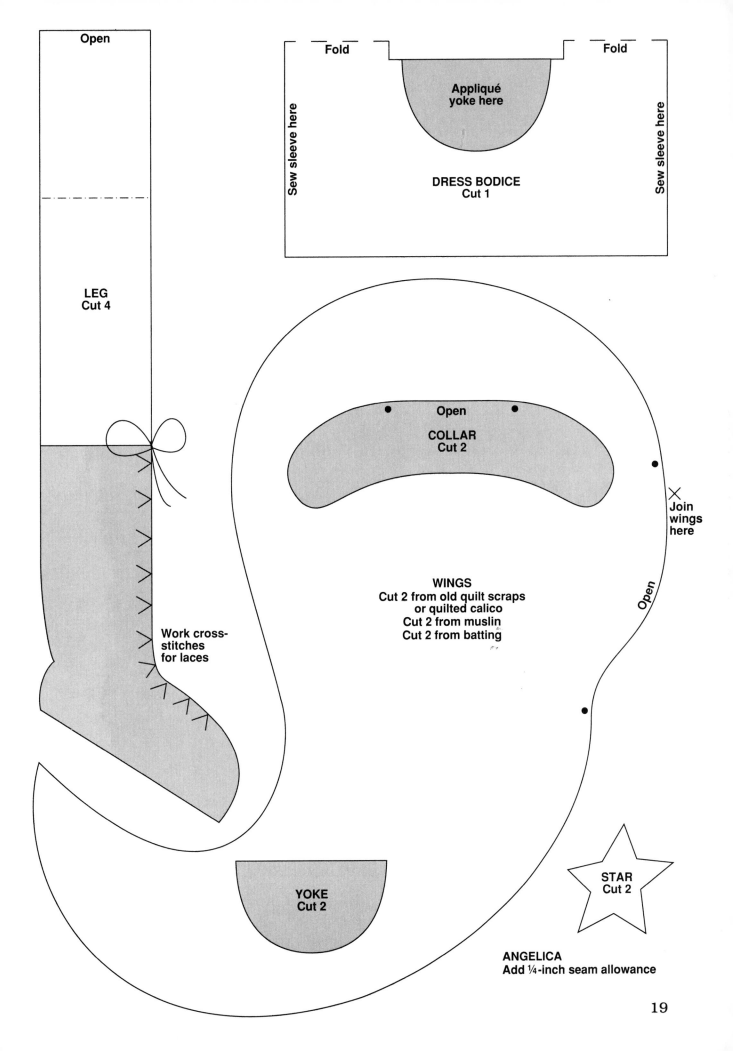

Open

LEG
Cut 4

Open

Fold

Fold

Sew sleeve here

Sew sleeve here

Appliqué
yoke here

DRESS BODICE
Cut 1

Open

COLLAR
Cut 2

Join
wings
here

Open

WINGS
Cut 2 from old quilt scraps
or quilted calico
Cut 2 from muslin
Cut 2 from batting

Work cross-
stitches
for laces

YOKE
Cut 2

STAR
Cut 2

ANGELICA
Add ¼-inch seam allowance

19

A BEAUTIFUL BRIDE

TO HAVE
AND TO HOLD

A wedding is a glorious event that requires months of preparation. The dress and veil are carefully selected, and the cake and flowers are ordered weeks in advance. And then, in a fleeting moment, the hour comes and goes. Only the top of the cake remains intact. The beautiful dress is put into storage until a daughter or niece asks to wear it for her special day.

Craft this 17-inch-tall bride doll as a gift to commemorate a friend's or relative's wedding day. Adjust the embroidered facial features, hair color, and hair style to resemble the real bride.

Change the details on the gown to reflect the embellishments on the wedding dress now carefully tucked away in the cedar chest.

If the original gown is handmade, ask for leftover scraps of fabric and trims to make the doll's dress more authentic. If the gown has been purchased, visit the bridal department in better fabric stores for embroidered voile, heavy satins, and elegant lace.

Full-size patterns for the doll and dress shown here begin on page 22. Or, use your own creativity and make a one-of-a-kind bride doll using these patterns as a helpful guide.

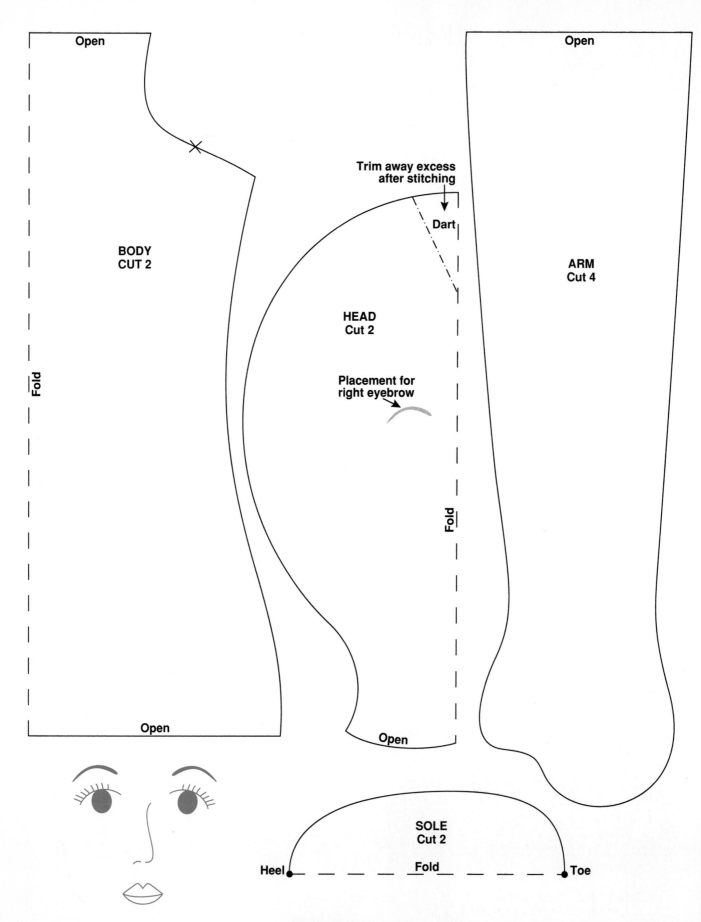

Open

BODY
CUT 2

Fold

Open

Open

Trim away excess
after stitching

Dart

ARM
Cut 4

HEAD
Cut 2

Placement for
right eyebrow

Fold

Open

SOLE
Cut 2

Heel   Fold   Toe

BRIDE DOLL
¼-inch seam allowance included

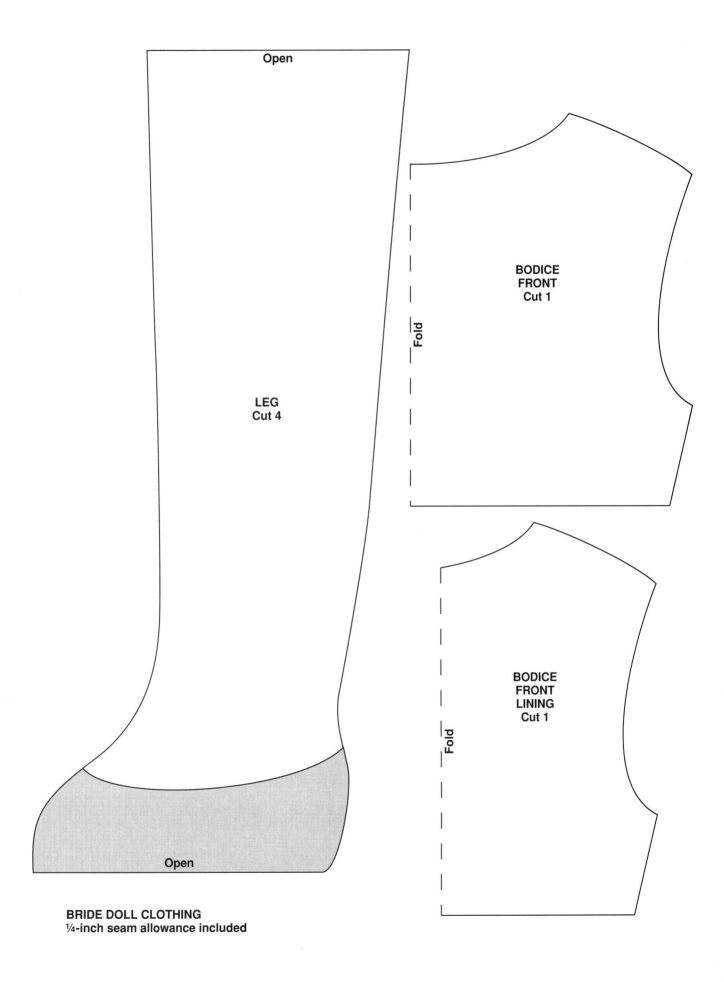

Open

LEG
Cut 4

Open

BODICE
FRONT
Cut 1

Fold

BODICE
FRONT
LINING
Cut 1

Fold

BRIDE DOLL CLOTHING
¼-inch seam allowance included

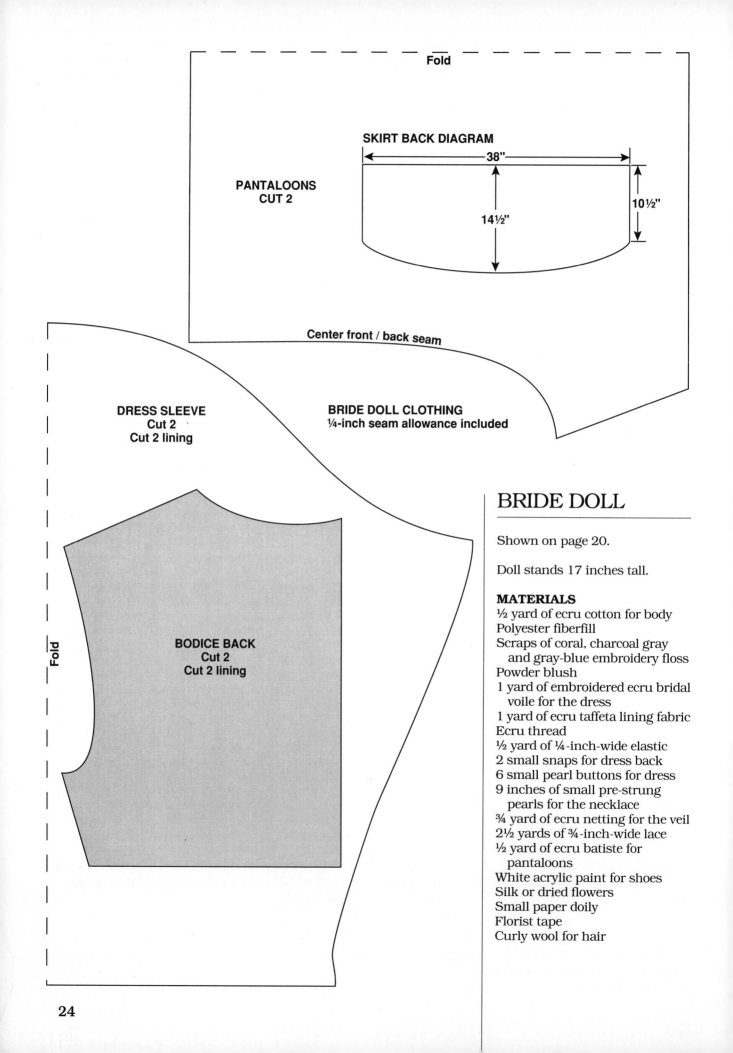

Fold

PANTALOONS
CUT 2

SKIRT BACK DIAGRAM

38"

14½"

10½"

Center front / back seam

DRESS SLEEVE
Cut 2
Cut 2 lining

BRIDE DOLL CLOTHING
¼-inch seam allowance included

Fold

BODICE BACK
Cut 2
Cut 2 lining

BRIDE DOLL

Shown on page 20.

Doll stands 17 inches tall.

MATERIALS
½ yard of ecru cotton for body
Polyester fiberfill
Scraps of coral, charcoal gray
    and gray-blue embroidery floss
Powder blush
1 yard of embroidered ecru bridal
    voile for the dress
1 yard of ecru taffeta lining fabric
Ecru thread
½ yard of ¼-inch-wide elastic
2 small snaps for dress back
6 small pearl buttons for dress
9 inches of small pre-strung
    pearls for the necklace
¾ yard of ecru netting for the veil
2½ yards of ¾-inch-wide lace
½ yard of ecru batiste for
    pantaloons
White acrylic paint for shoes
Silk or dried flowers
Small paper doily
Florist tape
Curly wool for hair

INSTRUCTIONS

Trace the patterns on pages 22–24 onto tracing paper and cut them out. Use ¼-inch seams on all stitching.

Solid lines on patterns are cutting lines; broken lines indicate where a pattern piece is placed on the fabric fold for cutting. Lines that alternate dots and dashes indicate a stitch line (darts, special topstitching). Embroidery stitch outlines appear in blue.

Draw one head piece onto cotton for the head front. Trace the face on page 22 onto the head front. Do not cut out the piece until the face is embroidered.

To embroider the face

Use two strands of floss and stitch diagrams on page 58 for embroidery. Use coral floss and satin stitches for the mouth. Use charcoal gray floss and satin stitches for eyebrows and top eyelids. Use charcoal gray and straight stitches for eyelashes. Use charcoal gray and the outline stitch for the nose. Use gray-blue floss and satin stitches for eyes.

Cut out the head front piece; press on the back side.

To make the body

Cut the body, head back, legs, soles of feet, and arm pieces from cotton fabric.

LEGS: With right sides facing, sew leg pieces together in sets, leaving top and bottom edges open. With right sides facing, match heel and toe dots on sole to dots on foot; baste. Machine-stitch sole to foot. Repeat for second leg. Clip curves and turn legs right side out. Stuff firmly with fiberfill to within 1 inch of top. Set aside.

ARMS: With right sides facing, sew arm pieces together in sets, leaving top edge open; clip curves. Turn right side out. Stuff with fiberfill to within 1 inch of top.

HEAD: Sew dart at top of head front and back pieces; trim darts close to seams. With right sides facing, sew front and back of head together, leaving neck edge open. Clip curves and turn right side out. Stuff firmly.

BODY: With right sides facing, sew the two body pieces together, leaving neck and across the bottom open. Turn body right side out. Turn bottom edge under ¼ inch. Insert legs into body with feet pointing forward. Stitch across bottom of body through all layers. Stuff the body firmly.

Turn neck edge under ¼ inch. Slip head into neck opening, matching side seams. Slip-stitch head to body.

Turn arm edges under ¼ inch. Gather the top of each arm to measure ¾ inch across and stitch to body, with thumbs pointing up, at X marking on pattern.

HAIR: The hair used on the doll on page 20 is from All Cooped Up, 560 S. State, No. B1, Orem, UT 84058. It is 100 percent wool and comes in a braid that when unraveled looks like wavy hair.

Glue or hand-stitch the hair in place on the doll's head in the desired hairstyle. Trim to shape.

To make the clothing

Cut bodice front, bodice back, and sleeve pieces from embroidered voile. Cut bodice front and back linings and sleeve lining from taffeta. Cut pantaloons from batiste.

Cut one 10½x20-inch rectangle from embroidered voile for skirt front. For skirt back, cut a rectangle that is 38 inches wide, 14½ inches deep in the middle (for the train), and 10½ inches on each side. (See Skirt Back Diagram, *opposite.*) Cut matching skirt pieces from the taffeta.

DRESS: Sew bodice front to back pieces at shoulder and side seams. Repeat for lining.

Gather neck edge and waist of bodice front to match bodice lining front. With right sides facing, sew bodice to lining along center back edges and around neckline. Clip curves. Turn and press.

With right sides facing, sew sleeve lining to sleeve along bottom (cuff) edge. Turn; press flat. Machine-stitch ⅜ inch in from edge of sleeve to form a casing. Insert elastic through casing and pull to fit doll's wrist. Tack in place at each end to hold.

With right sides facing, sew sleeve underarm seam. Gather top edge to fit bodice arm opening; baste in place, pulling gathers to top of sleeve. With right sides facing, sew sleeve to bodice.

Stitch ecru lace to bodice neckline for a collar. With right sides facing, stitch skirt front and backs together at the side seams. Make a 2-inch slit at the center back of the waist. Turn the raw edges of the fabric slit to the inside and stitch. Repeat for lining.

Hem dress skirt and dress skirt lining. Machine-stitch lace to bottom of skirt. With wrong side of dress skirt lying on top of right side of lining, gather the two together at the waistline to fit the bodice. With right sides together, stitch lined skirt to bodice.

Sew small buttons and snaps at back opening. Place dress on doll.

SASH: Cut a 3x36-inch rectangle from taffeta. Hem all sides. Fold ends to form V-shape and hand-stitch. Tie around doll's waist.

PANTALOONS: Hem legs; trim with ecru lace. With right sides facing, sew pieces together along the center front/back seam. Turn under ½ inch twice along waistline to form a casing; machine-stitch, leaving an opening to insert elastic. Cut elastic to fit doll's waist; insert elastic through the casing and secure ends with thread. Sew inner leg seams.

VEIL: Cut a 10-inch-, 11-inch-, and 12-inch-diameter circle from netting. Gather 8 inches along the edge of each circle and attach in layers to the underside of a 3-inch-long piece of lace. Pin in place on the doll's head.

SHOES: Paint shoe area defined on leg pattern with white acrylic paint. Glue a small piece of lace to the top of each shoe.

FINISHING: Place pearls around neck. Add powder blush to face.

25

NATURAL BEAUTIES

FOUND OBJECTS

Taking a fanciful cue from Mother Nature, these handcrafted dolls conjure up true country enchantment wherever they go. Whether they star in a sentimental showcase of antique collectibles, or go solo as folk art, they'll win your heart and add something-special personality to any room. For dolls in this chapter, gather materials from the scrap bag, the attic, country roadsides, and gardens. Your imagination brings them to life.

Carrying on the creative—and frugal— traditions of generations of country dollmakers, the prissy pair of piano players, *right,* is the product of a variety of leftovers.

Gussied up in pretty fabric scraps, snippets of ribbon, bits of fur and stray buttons, Clara Mae (left) and Hester (right) have been royally coiffed in curly wool, dried weeds, and other natural pickings.

A few quick brush strokes with latex and acrylic paints add comical expressions, flashy nail color, and saucy red or more conservative black high- heeled shoes.

The real fun begins long before the assembly as you forage through sewing baskets, jewelry boxes, forgotten drawers, and antiques shops for fabrics and trims.

And, there's just no end to the materials that nature provides each season with pods and berries, cones, and dried foliage. A list of suggestions is on page 36, but use anything you find that appeals to your creative senses.

The wonderful antique doll furniture in the photograph may fool you, but our ladies are not 5 feet tall. Each doll is only 13 inches in height.

Patterns and instructions for these dolls begin on page 32.

No matter how humble the on-hand materials, yesterday's doll artists worked magic with them, creating homespun dolls that, today, enjoy folk-art status in homes from rustic to contemporary.

Primped in an array of naturals, Gloria and Lucille, *opposite,* discuss their weekend plans over a cup of tea. Gloria (right) seems quite content to spend her days by the shore, collecting tiny shells to embellish her hair and wardrobe. Her friend, Lucille (left), all decked out in tiny flags as she stands in patriotic salute, anxiously waits for her ship to come in.

As you can see from the photograph, *above,* Prudence now has every pod-and-cone curl in place and finally is ready to join her friends for an afternoon of harmless gossip.

Norfolk Island pinecones, Spanish moss, baby's-breath, pea pods, and cinnamon fern fronds make each 14-inch muslin doll a one-of-a-kind collector's item. All three dolls are fashioned from one simple pattern.

Instructions begin on page 34.

Lovingly fashioned from pick-of-the-harvest materials, corn-husk and apple-head dolls are always a delight for the country doll collector.

Constance, our corn-husk belle, *above,* can be dressed in any combination of colors. Natural corn husks are shaped while they are wet to form the 8-inch doll. They are dyed for the pinafore, hat, and hair bow.

Granny Smith, *opposite,* doesn't have wrinkles—those are just laugh lines. Simple carving of the apple will help define the nose, mouth, chin, and ears. But, as each apple dries, it will take on its own one-of-a-kind expression. This 12-inch senior citizen is a real character and perfect for gift-giving.

Read through the instructions on page 38 to discover how simple to make corn-husk and apple-head dolls can be.

Clara Mae and Hester

Clara Mae is shown on page 26. Hester is shown on page 27.

Each doll stands 13 inches tall.

MATERIALS
For either doll
¼ yard of muslin for the doll body
Black print fabric for legs
Tracing paper
Pencil
Polyester fiberfill
Acrylic paints in the following colors: black, brown, white, blue, pink, and red
Gray latex enamel
Small paintbrushes
Knitting needle (or blunt-pointed object)
Crafts glue or glue gun

For Clara Mae
Scraps of black-and-white print fabric
Thread
5 inches of 1-inch-wide black velvet ribbon for the belt
Button for the belt buckle
8 inches of black fake fur for the stole
German statice, artemisia, grapevine curls, cockscomb, red canellas, or rose hips for the hair

For Hester
Scraps of two complementary purple print fabrics
Thread
2½ inches of ½-inch-wide lace for the collar
15 inches of 1-inch-wide satin ribbon for the sash
6 ⅜-inch-diameter buttons
Curly wool (lamb, goat, or llama) for hair
Purchased doll hat
Grapevine curls, pink pepper berries, globe amaranth, pods, and long-needle pine sprig for hat

INSTRUCTIONS
A ¼-inch seam allowance is included with each full-size pattern, *opposite*. Use ¼-inch seams when sewing all pieces together.

Solid lines on the patterns are cutting lines; arrows mark areas to be left open for turning and stuffing. Dashed lines on the hand pattern are stitching lines.

Facial features are shown in blue on the body/head pattern.

For the body
Trace the arm, leg, and head/body pattern pieces, *opposite*, onto tracing paper; cut out. Cut arms and head/body pieces from muslin; cut legs from black print.

With right sides facing, sew a pair of arms and a pair of legs, leaving the straight ends open for turning. Clip curves; turn right side out. Use a small knitting needle or blunt pointed object to push out the fingers and the shoe toe and heel. Stuff the finger area lightly with polyester fiberfill. Flatten and machine-stitch fingers on the hand. Stuff the thumb and arm. Stuff the legs.

With right sides facing, sew the head/body pieces together. Clip curves; turn right side out. Push out the nose and chin with a knitting needle or other blunt-end object; stuff with fiberfill.

Turn the raw edges of one arm to the inside. Hand-stitch the arm to the body at shoulder height with the thumb pointing in. (An X marking on the head/body pattern shows you where to attach the arm.) Repeat with the other arm.

Lay the doll down with the face pointing up. Stuff the head and body with fiberfill. Turn under the bottom raw edge of the body fabric. Insert the legs inside the doll body with the toes pointing up. Machine-stitch across the body, through all layers, securing the legs in place.

Paint the face, neck, body, and arms with gray latex enamel. (House paint works great.) Do not paint the doll's scalp.

Using a pencil and the drawing on the head/body pattern piece as a guide, draw a face on the doll. Using acrylic paints, paint eyebrows, eyelashes, and outline around the eyes brown. Paint the eyes blue, surrounded by white. Paint the mouth pink with a red line between the two lips. To add blush to the cheeks, put a small amount of pink paint on a wet, crumpled napkin and sponge the cheek area lightly.

Paint on fingernails with pink paint. Paint the shoes with two coats of red or black paint.

For the dresses
DRESS: Trace and cut two bodice pieces from print fabric. Cut two 3x4½-inch rectangles for sleeves. Cut one 4¼x12-inch rectangle for the skirt.

With right sides facing, sew together the bodice side seams, leaving the armhole areas open; leave the top and bottom open. Turn right side out. Sew buttons down the bodice front, if desired. Slip the bodice on the doll from the bottom of the doll body.

Fold one sleeve rectangle in half, right sides facing, and sew the 4½-inch edges together. Turn right side out. Hem one edge for the cuff. Turn the opposite edge under for the shoulder. Place sleeve on doll; hand-stitch sleeve to armhole opening of bodice. *Note:* Sleeve seam should match with bodice seam under the arm. Repeat for other sleeve rectangle.

With right sides facing, sew short ends of the skirt rectangle together. Hem one raw edge for bottom of skirt. Gather the top to fit the bodice. Slip the skirt onto the doll and adjust gathers; hand-stitch skirt to the bodice. Cover the gathered drop waist with 1-inch-wide ribbon. Tie in a bow at the back, or overlap ribbon in front and stitch a large decorative button at the overlap.

Run a gathering thread around the neck edge of the bodice and pull up gathers to fit the neck; tie knot to secure. Cover the neckline with lace edging, scraps of fur, or old jewelry. The more you decorate, the greater the character of the finished doll. Add whatever you like, using trinkets from old jewelry and odds and ends from scrap bags.

For Clara Mae's hair
The tip box on page 36 offers alternatives to natural materials used on doll on pages 26 and 27.

Glue small sprigs of German statice and artemisia to the head a little at a time. Fill in with grapevine curls, dried cockscomb, red canellas, or rose hips. (Remember that you cannot overdo the hair.)
continued

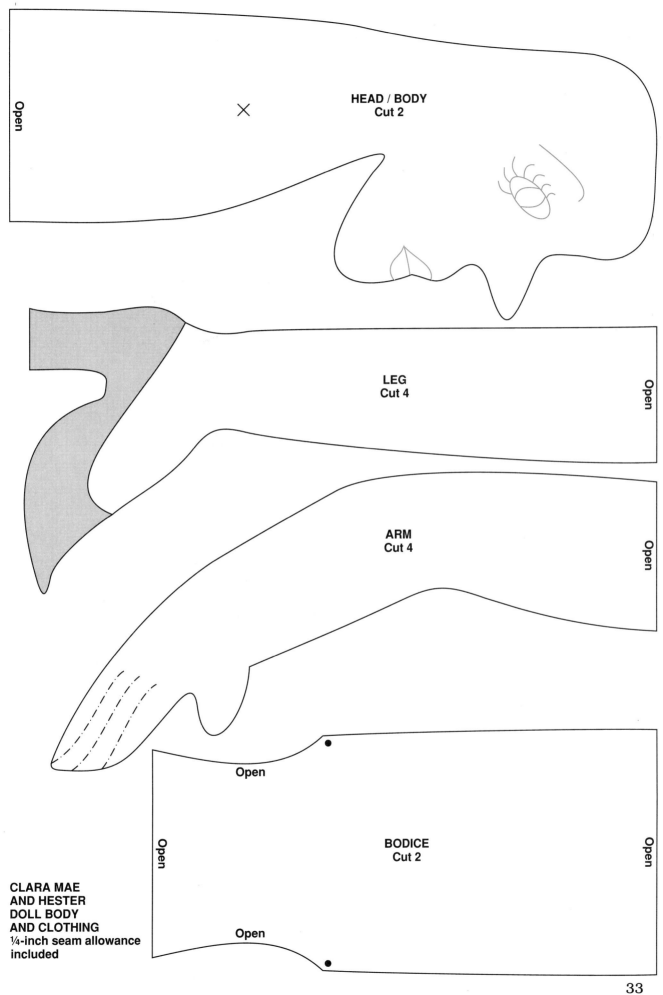

Open

HEAD / BODY
Cut 2

LEG
Cut 4

Open

ARM
Cut 4

Open

Open

BODICE
Cut 2

Open

Open

Open

CLARA MAE
AND HESTER
DOLL BODY
AND CLOTHING
¼-inch seam allowance
included

For Hester's hair

Glue curly wool all over the head. Glue a purchased doll hat in place. Decorate the hat with grapevine curls, pink pepper berries, globe amaranth, pods, and a sprig of long-needle pine.

For suggestions for other naturals to use on the doll's head, see the tip box on page 36.

Gloria, Lucille, and Prudence

Shown on pages 28 and 29.

Each doll stands 14 inches tall.

MATERIALS
For one doll
¼ yard of muslin fabric for the body
Scrap of black or brown cotton for legs
Tracing paper
Pencil
Polyester fiberfill
Knitting needle or blunt-pointed object
Crafts glue or glue gun

For Gloria
Scraps of taffeta or moiré for the dress
8 inches of 1-inch-wide satin ribbon for the belt
15 inches of ¼-inch-wide satin ribbon for the hair bow
6-inch-square fabric doily
1 old button with a colored stone
12 small seashells
Norfolk Island pinecones
Small pods
Small twigs
Grapevine curls

For Lucille
Scraps of navy wool for the dress
Scraps of white cotton twill for the collar
5 inches of 1½-inch-wide red satin ribbon for the bow
Red acrylic paint for the stars on the collar
3 paper flags approximately ⅞x1⅜ inches
Spanish moss
Small seashells
Small pods

For Prudence
Scraps of two contrasting print fabrics for the dress and apron
18 inches of 1-inch-wide velvet ribbon for the apron belt
4 old decorative buttons
Dried creeping baby's-breath
Dried pea pods
Small round pods
Cinnamon fern
Dried cones
Small twigs

INSTRUCTIONS
For the body of all three dolls
A ¼-inch seam allowance has been included with each pattern . Use ¼-inch seams for all sewing. Solid lines on the pattern are cutting lines; dashed lines indicate where a pattern piece is placed on the fold for cutting.

Trace the full-size head/body pattern, *opposite,* and the arm and leg patterns on page 36 onto tracing paper; cut out. Pin head/body and arm patterns to muslin fabric and cut out the required number of pieces. Cut legs from black or brown fabric.

With right sides facing, sew a pair of arms and a pair of legs, leaving the straight ends open for turning. Clip curves; turn pieces right side out. Use a small knitting needle or blunt-pointed object to push out the fingers and the shoe toe and heel. Stuff arms and legs with polyester fiberfill.

With right sides facing, sew the head/body pieces together. Leave open the bottom and the openings between the dots (for the arms) that are marked on the pattern. Clip curves; turn right side out.

Turn under the armhole openings of the body. Place the arms in the armholes, thumbs pointing down, and machine-stitch across the opening.

Lay the doll down with the face pointing up. Stuff the body with fiberfill. Turn under the bottom edges of the body fabric. Insert the legs inside the doll body with the toes pointing up. Machine-stitch across the body, securing the legs in place.

For Gloria's clothing
Trace the full-size sleeve and short bodice patterns on page 37 onto tracing paper; cut out. Pin the patterns to taffeta or moiré fabric. Cut two sleeves and two short bodices. Cut two 7x8-inch rectangles for the skirt.

Gather a 7-inch edge of one rectangle and adjust the gathers to fit the bottom edge of one bodice piece. Repeat for the second skirt rectangle and bodice piece. With right sides facing, sew the two bodice shoulder seams together. Leave the neck edge open.

Use small running stitches to gather the sleeves along the shoulder edges. Lay the dress open flat. With right sides facing, pin the sleeves to the dress at the arm openings, adjusting the gathers to fit. Machine-stitch the sleeves in place.

With right sides facing, pin the dress pieces together. Sew the dress together. Start at the sleeve cuff and stitch down the inside of the sleeve and then down the side of the bodice and skirt. Press the seams open. Hem the skirt.

Place the dress on the body. If the neck opening seems too small for the head, cut several small slits at the back of the neckline. Turn the neck edge and cuffs under ¼ inch and tack in place.

Center and tack 8 inches of 1-inch-wide ribbon over the waistline, overlapping the ends in back; hand-tack the ends in place.

Cut an opening in the center of a 6-inch-square doily to match the neckline. Stitch the raw edges under at the neckline; slip the doily over the doll's head. Trim the doily collar with buttons and shells. *Note:* If you do not have a small doily, you can cut an interesting collar from a larger fabric doily and hem it on all sides to measure 6 inches. Or, you may use a scrap from an old quilt top or any other piece of fabric to make the 6-inch-square collar.

For Gloria's hair
Natural materials given are only suggestions. Other ideas are listed in the tip box on page 36.

Glue Norfolk Island pinecones along the back of the head, starting at the bottom. Layer the cones upward a little at a time. Decorate the top of the head with small cones, pods, shells, sticks, and vines. Add a small ribbon bow.

For Prudence's clothing

Trace the sleeve and short bodice patterns on page 37 onto tracing paper; cut out.

Cut two sleeves and two short bodices from cotton print fabric. Cut two 7x8-inch rectangles from the same print for the skirt. Cut one 7x16-inch rectangle from contrasting fabric for the apron.

Assemble dress following the directions for Gloria's clothing, *opposite*.

Hem one long side of the apron rectangle and both short sides. Gather the remaining long edge to approximately 6 inches. Hand-stitch the apron to the dress at the waistline. Center and position an 18-inch length of 1-inch-wide ribbon over the apron and tie it in a bow at the back of the dress.

Glue or sew old buttons at the neckline of the dress.

Flatten a small pinecone with a hammer. Fold a 15-inch length of ¼-inch-wide ribbon in half. Tie the ends into a bow, leaving the folded loop open to fit over the doll's hands. Using crafts glue or a glue gun, glue the center of the bow to the top of the flattened pinecone, making the doll's purse.

For Prudence's hair

Glue a layer of dried creeping baby's-breath on the doll's head. Use small bunches of baby's-breath and work around the back and top of the head. Glue in dried pea pods, cinnamon fern fronds, cones, pods, and sticks until you are satisfied with the shape of the hair. Add smaller naturals to cover open areas.

For Lucille's clothing

Trace the full-size sleeve, middy front, middy back, and middy collar patterns on page 37 onto tracing paper; cut out.

From the wool, cut two sleeves, one middy front, one middy back, and two 5x7-inch rectangles for the skirt. Cut two middy collars from the white twill.

Assemble using the directions for Gloria's clothing, *opposite*.

Place the dress on the doll body with the V-opening in the front.

continued

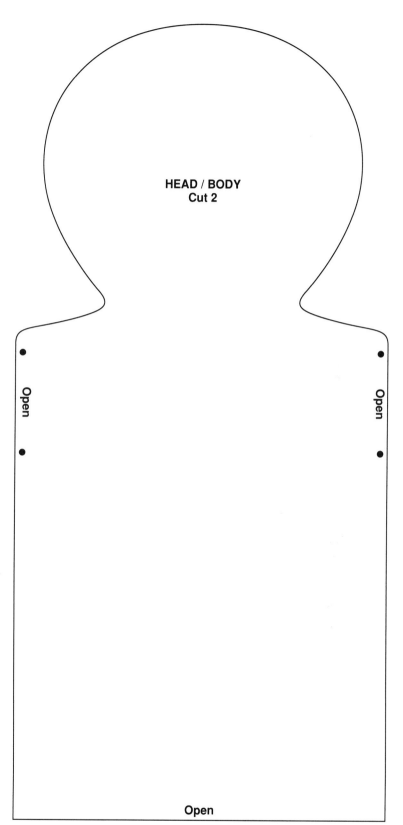

HEAD / BODY
Cut 2

Open

Open

Open

GLORIA, LUCILLE, AND PRUDENCE DOLL BODY
¼-inch seam allowance included

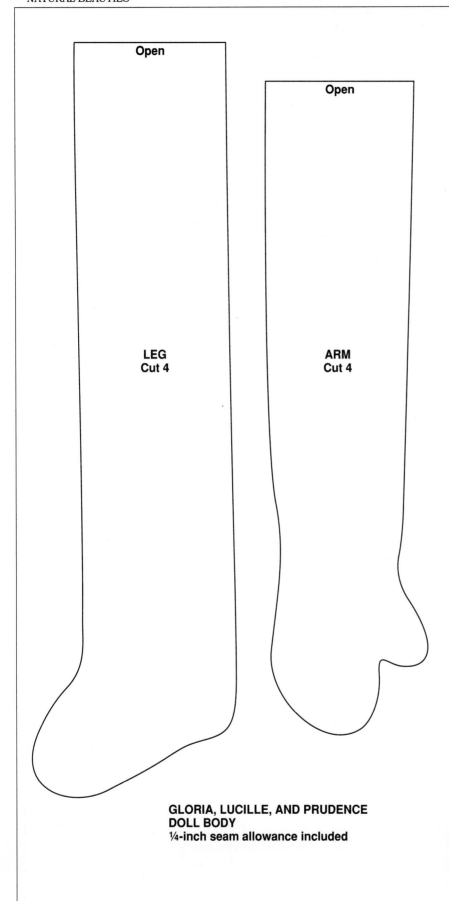

Open

Open

LEG
Cut 4

ARM
Cut 4

**GLORIA, LUCILLE, AND PRUDENCE
DOLL BODY**
¼-inch seam allowance included

Turn the neck edge and cuffs under ¼ inch and sew in place. With right sides facing, sew the two middy collar pieces together, leaving a small opening at the back of the neck for turning. Clip curves. Turn the collar right side out; sew the opening closed and press flat. Topstitch around the entire collar ¼ inch from the edge. Paint red stars in the front corners. (Refer to the photograph on page 28 for guidance.)

Place the collar over the doll's head; hand-stitch in place. Add a red bow made from 1-inch-wide satin ribbon.

For Lucille's hair
Glue Spanish moss over the entire scalp. Glue small shells and pods around the face. Glue paper flags in place, referring to the photograph on page 28 for guidance. Tack the doll's hand to her forehead in a salute position.

Trimming Dolls With Natural Materials

No matter what part of the country you call home, there is a variety of dried pods, cones, sticks, and other wonderful crafting supplies that nature has shed.

If the material has dried naturally, it will not mold, mildew, or collect bugs. Dry all materials in the sun, if possible.

Following are suggestions of natural materials that will make each doll uniquely yours.

Annual statice
Artemisia
Baby's-breath
Canellas
Cinnamon fern
Cockscomb
Dried pea pods
Field weeds
German statice
Globe amaranth
Pepper berries
Rose hips
Shells
Small pinecones and pods
Spanish moss
Sticks
Stones
Tree bark
Vine curls

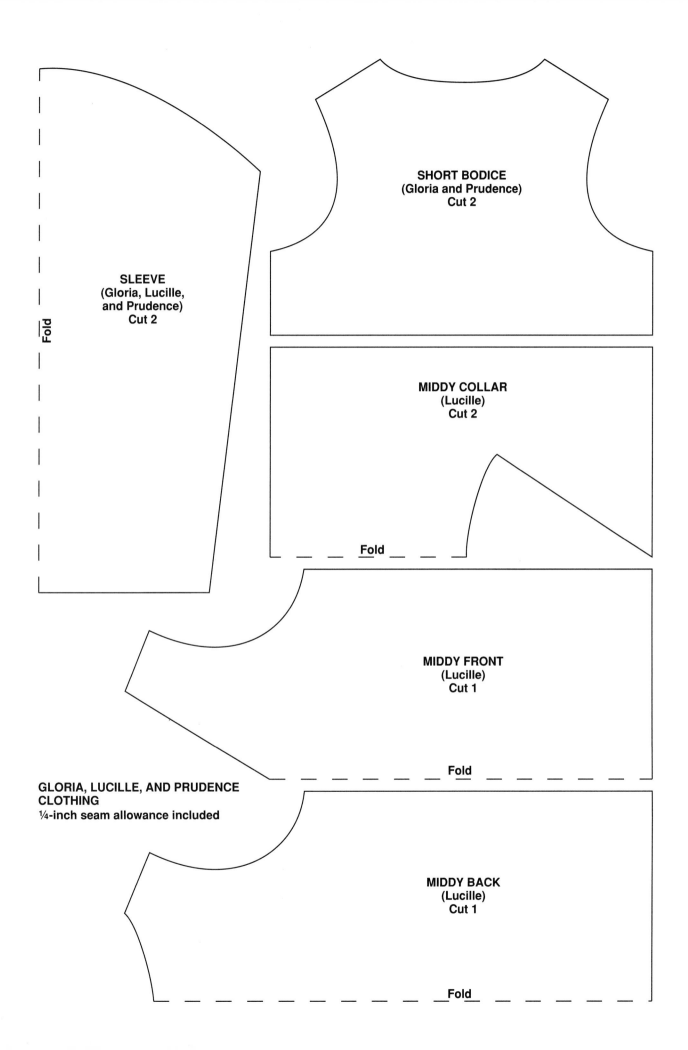

SHORT BODICE
(Gloria and Prudence)
Cut 2

SLEEVE
(Gloria, Lucille,
and Prudence)
Cut 2

Fold

MIDDY COLLAR
(Lucille)
Cut 2

Fold

MIDDY FRONT
(Lucille)
Cut 1

Fold

GLORIA, LUCILLE, AND PRUDENCE
CLOTHING
¼-inch seam allowance included

MIDDY BACK
(Lucille)
Cut 1

Fold

Constance

Shown on page 30.

Doll stands 8 inches tall.

MATERIALS
18 corn husks, each approximately 6 inches wide
Blue, red, and brown fabric dyes
Straight pins
Crafts glue
Thread
Two ¾-inch plastic foam balls
12 inches of 19-gauge wire
Wire cutters
Cotton balls
Masking tape

INSTRUCTIONS
Preparing the husks
Soak all husks in warm soapy water; rinse. Work with husks while they are wet. For colored husks, dip in boiling fabric dye, rinse in cold water. Dye one husk brown, one red, and seven blue. Leave nine husks natural. *Note:* You will have greater control over the lightness or darkness of the color if husks have been soaked in warm water before they are dipped in the boiling fabric dye. Check the husks often until they reach the desired color.

For the head and arms
Cut off a 6-inch piece of wire and insert it through the center of one plastic foam ball. Bend ¼ inch of one end of the wire to keep it from pulling out of the ball (top of the head); push the ball to that end of the wire. Cover the ball with one natural-colored corn husk, pulling the husk together at the bottom of the ball. Wrap thread around the husk at the base of the ball.

Cut off a piece of wire 6 inches long for the arms; at both ends, form oval loops that measure about ½-inch long and ¼-inch wide for the hands. Wrap small pieces of natural-colored husk around the loops. Continue wrapping husks to the middle of the 6-inch piece of wire. Secure the husks around the wire with thread.

For sleeves, gather a 3-inch-wide strip of natural corn husk around each wrist, extending the husk backward over the hand as you work. Wrap the ends with thread to secure. Pull the husks back and up over the wrapped arm pieces to form puffy sleeves.

Wrap husks for both sleeves with thread near the center of the wire (shoulders). Position the center at the base of the head; wrap with thread to secure.

For the dress collar
The collar is added before going on to the chest.

For the collar, lay one natural corn husk on one side of the neck; fold it up over the head. Repeat with a second corn husk along the other side of the head. Wrap the husks with thread about $\frac{1}{16}$ inch from the head.

For the chest and waist
Place two cotton balls in the center of a natural-colored corn husk; fold the long edges toward the center, covering the cotton balls. Fold the husk in half crosswise, matching the two short ends. Wrap thread around the husk just below the cotton balls to shape the waist. Place on the head wire approximately ½ inch below the head. This will leave a neck area between the chest and head. Wrap thread over the shoulders and around the waist to join the pieces.

Center a ½-inch piece of blue corn husk over each shoulder. Cross the husks in front and back, gathering them at the waist to form the bodice; secure them at the waist with thread.

To make the hair
Form a loop with 1-inch-wide brown corn husk and secure at the raw end with thread. Clip the looped end into ⅛-inch-wide sections. Make four such pieces. Allow the husk to dry. When the husk is dry, clip off the tied end. Pin and glue the curls to the head.

To finish the clothing
Fold the collar down over the shoulders and cut a rounded shape. Refer to the photograph on page 30 for guidance. Pin the collar in place until the husk is dry.

SKIRT: Layer six blue husks from the waist area up and over the doll's head; secure with thread at the waist. Cut six natural husks in half widthwise. Layer natural husks on top of blue husks and secure with thread.

Pull natural and blue husks down to form skirt; pin husks in place. For the curl on the skirt, make a 1-inch-diameter tube from cardboard. Wrap skirt edges around the tube; secure with hair pins until husks are dry. While husks are still wet, trim the bottom of the skirt evenly.

HAT: Mold a 3-inch circle of blue corn husk over a foam ball. Slightly below halfway, wrap the ball loosely with thread. Curl one edge (brim) back over a pencil and tape in place. Trim the back edge closer to the crown to form the hat shape. Dry thoroughly. Remove the thread and tape. Glue the hat to the head.

BOW: Cut a 6-inch length of red husk ⅛-inch wide. Tie in a bow and glue to dress neckline.

Granny Smith

Shown on page 31.

Doll stands 12 inches tall.

MATERIALS
Cornstarch
White glue
Two large apples
Salt
Lemon
Carving knife
19-gauge wire
Thread
Fiberfill
8x14-inch piece of thin cardboard
Masking tape
Blue check and red print fabric scraps for clothing
Muslin scraps for the apron
Paper towels
Unspun wool for hair
Red acrylic paint
Powder blush
Five pearl beads for earrings and buttons on blouse
Tracing paper

INSTRUCTIONS
For the doll

EYES: Mix cornstarch and glue together until you have a consistency you can knead as you would dough. Form the dough into shapes that are 3/16 inch on one end and rounded like an eyeball. Taper the other end to a point that will stick into the apple head. Bake these shapes in an oven for one to two hours (or until dry) at 175 degrees.

HEAD: In a shallow bowl, put water just deep enough to cover the apple you are carving. Add 2 tablespoons of salt and the juice from one lemon; mix well. Peel the apple. Dip the apple into the water mixture often as you carve the features. Refer to the photograph on page 31 for guidance, but keep in mind that no two apple-head dolls will ever be the same. Each apple is going to shrink and dry differently than the next. Your carving will only ensure definite eye sockets, ears, chin, and nose features.

When carving is finished, hollow out the center of the apple. Sprinkle the inside and outside of the carved apple with salt. Push the eyes in place in the sockets. Place a stick through the center of the apple and lay the stick across the sides of a bowl, making certain the apple does not touch the bowl. Let apple dry for 62 hours in an oven that is 175 degrees.

ALTERNATE DRYING METHOD: The apple also may be air-dried naturally for 4 weeks. Run a wire, string, or stick through the center and hang to dry. Do *not* hang in the sun or near a heat register. The heat will *not* promote drying and only will discolor the apple.

HANDS AND WRIST: Carve hands and wrists from the second apple following the instructions, *above.* Leave 1 inch for the wrist, and let the hands dry with the apple head by hanging them from the oven rack or air-drying.

FACE: Apply a small amount of red acrylic paint to lips, and brush powder blush on the cheeks. Glue pearls to ears for earrings.

NECK: Cut one piece of wire 8 inches long. Make a loop at one end. The loop will be at the top of the neck. Wrap fiberfill around the top end until you have a thickness equal to the opening in the base of the apple head and about 1 inch long. Secure the fiberfill with thread. Coat the top half of the fiberfill with glue and insert it into the base of the head. Squeeze a small amount of glue onto the area where the head and neck connect and allow the glue to dry thoroughly.

ARMS: Cut a piece of wire 12 inches long. Wrap the wire with fiberfill and secure the fiberfill to the wire with thread. Leave 1 inch of bare wire on each end of the arms. Stick the wire through the wrists of the apple hands and form a loop around the top of the wrists so that the hands do not come off. Coat the upper 1/2 inch of the wrist with glue. Wrap the upper part of the wrists where the wire is attached with fiberfill. Fasten in place with thread.

TORSO: Stick the wire from the head through the center of the fiberfill covered arms. Wrap thread around neck and shoulders to secure. Wrap fiberfill around the torso area to fill out the bodice area to the desired thickness and the waist to 2½ inches. Wrap an additional 2 inches below the waist; wrap with thread to secure.

BASE: Roll the cardboard piece into a cone 8 inches deep, 4½ inches in diameter at the base, and 2¼ inches in diameter at the top. Coat the batting-covered torso with glue and insert the torso into the cardboard cone. Trim the bottom of the cone so that the cone is level and measures 7 inches in depth.

HAIR: Squeeze a line of glue along the hairline. Lay wool from hairline over the face and press the ends into the glue. Allow the glue to dry thoroughly. Pull the wool back and form it into a bun on top of the head.

For the clothing

A ¼-inch seam allowance has been included with each full-size pattern on pages 40 and 41. Use ¼-inch seams on all stitching. Solid lines on pattern are cutting lines; dashed lines indicate where a pattern is placed on the fabric fold for cutting.

BLOUSE: Transfer patterns on pages 40 and 41 onto tracing paper; cut out patterns. Cut pieces from red print fabric.

With right sides facing, sew blouse back to fronts at shoulder seams. Turn edge of fronts under ¼ inch and topstitch. (Blouse will be overlapped and stitched to doll on completion.)

Cut a 3¾x1-inch strip of red print fabric for the collar; fold in half lengthwise with right sides facing and sew across short ends. Turn collar right side out and press flat. Lay the collar strip, right sides together and raw edges matching, against the blouse neckline; stitch in place. Clip curves; turn collar upward and press.

With right sides facing, sew sleeves to blouse at armhole openings. Clip curves. Stitch underarms and side seams. Turn sleeve under at wrist and hand-gather around wrist with thread and needle; knot to secure.

Sew three pearl buttons to right side of blouse front. Place on doll and overlap front pieces with right side on top. Hand-stitch blouse front closed at collar and waist.

JUMPER: To make the jumper, align the AB markings on the two pattern halves (pages 40 and 41) and cut one complete pattern from tracing paper. Cut one jumper bodice facing pattern using only the shaded area on the jumper pattern.

Cut jumper from blue print. With right sides together, sew one bodice facing to each jumper front/back piece. Leave bottom open. Turn right side out and press.

Sew sides of jumper together. Stitch ¼-inch hem at bottom. Slip over doll's head and hand-stitch together at shoulders, overlapping shoulder straps.

continued

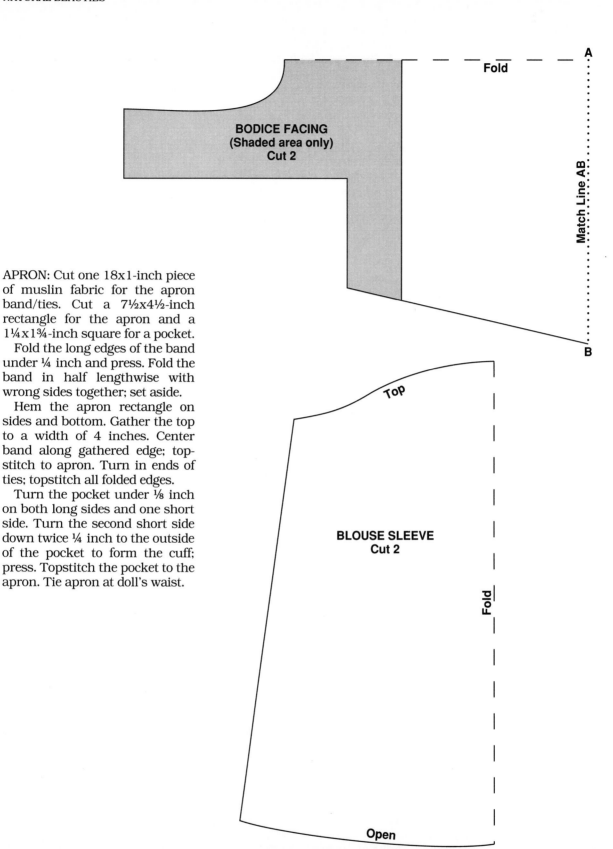

APRON: Cut one 18x1-inch piece of muslin fabric for the apron band/ties. Cut a 7½x4½-inch rectangle for the apron and a 1¼x1¾-inch square for a pocket.

Fold the long edges of the band under ¼ inch and press. Fold the band in half lengthwise with wrong sides together; set aside.

Hem the apron rectangle on sides and bottom. Gather the top to a width of 4 inches. Center band along gathered edge; topstitch to apron. Turn in ends of ties; topstitch all folded edges.

Turn the pocket under ⅛ inch on both long sides and one short side. Turn the second short side down twice ¼ inch to the outside of the pocket to form the cuff; press. Topstitch the pocket to the apron. Tie apron at doll's waist.

GRANNY SMITH CLOTHING
¼-inch seam allowance included

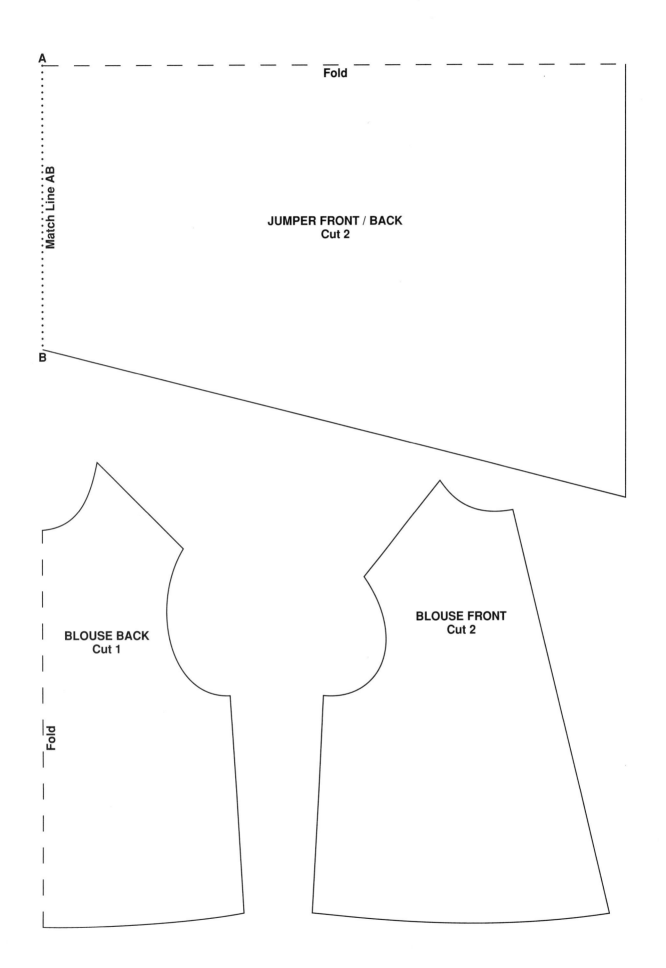

A

Fold

Match Line AB

B

JUMPER FRONT / BACK
Cut 2

BLOUSE BACK
Cut 1

Fold

BLOUSE FRONT
Cut 2

UNCLE SAM, LADY LIBERTY

♦ ♦ ♦

Dressed in Old Glory's stars and bars, this all-American couple will draw cheers of praise from any crowd. You don't have to be a skilled woodworker to craft this patriotic pair. The simple shapes are quick and easy to cut with the help of a bandsaw.

Folk-art figures like the Uncle Sam and Lady Liberty, *left,* symbolize a nation of proud Americans for many and are favorites in country decorating schemes.

Salute your own crafting abilities when you see how simple it is to achieve the same spectacular results in your basement workshop.

The 20-inch Uncle Sam and the 16½-inch Lady Liberty each start with a 2½-inch-diameter post. Small pieces of wood cut from the post are used for arms and noses.

Sam's shoes are cast from modeling compound, his coat from black felt, and his hair from curly wool. Smaller scraps of wood are used for his hat and star-spangled base.

Liberty's flag has been tea-dyed to match the ivory stars and stripes in her dress. Bits of plywood cut into star shapes create her crown.

Acrylic paints of red, gold, navy, and ivory add the detail and create the spirit in this pair.

Instructions and exploded diagrams for easy assembly begin on page 44.

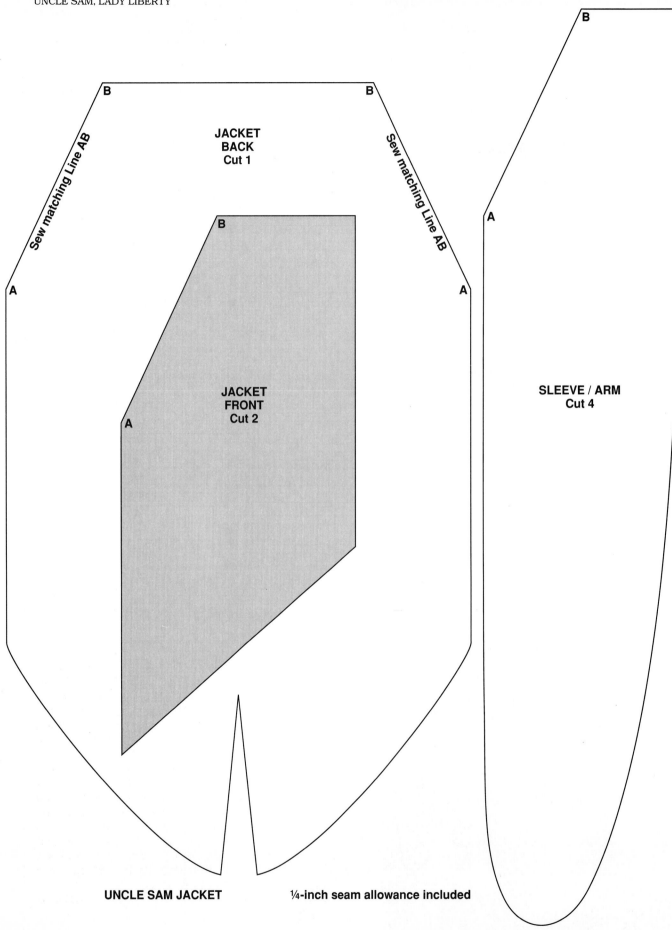

JACKET BACK Cut 1

Sew matching Line AB

Sew matching Line AB

JACKET FRONT Cut 2

SLEEVE / ARM Cut 4

UNCLE SAM JACKET ¼-inch seam allowance included

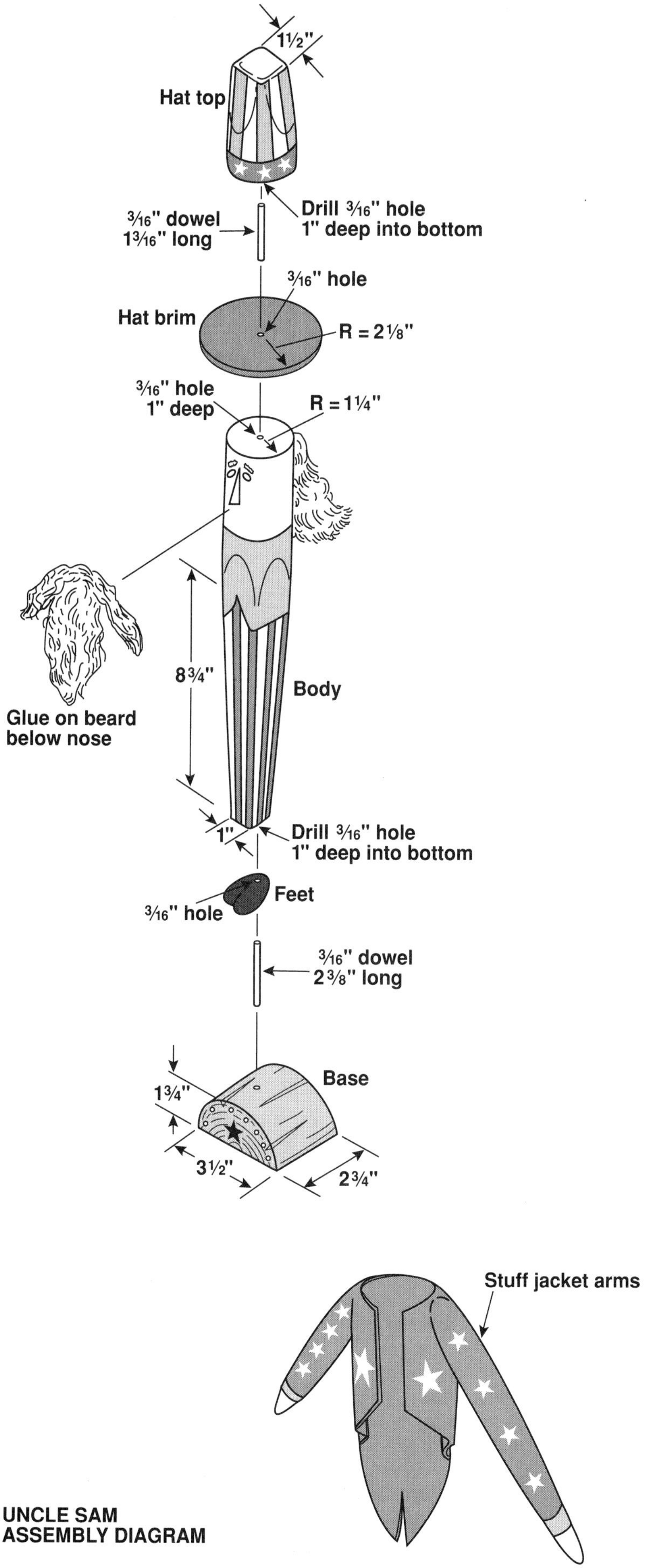

Diagram labels (left)

1½"

Hat top

³⁄₁₆" dowel
1³⁄₁₆" long

**Drill ³⁄₁₆" hole
1" deep into bottom**

³⁄₁₆" hole

Hat brim

R = 2⅛"

³⁄₁₆" hole
1" deep

R = 1¼"

8¾"

Body

**Glue on beard
below nose**

1"

**Drill ³⁄₁₆" hole
1" deep into bottom**

Feet

³⁄₁₆" hole

³⁄₁₆" dowel
2⅜" long

1¾"

Base

3½"

2¾"

Stuff jacket arms

**UNCLE SAM
ASSEMBLY DIAGRAM**

Uncle Sam

Shown on page 42.

Finished height of Uncle Sam is 20 inches.

MATERIALS
Wool or synthetic hair
17-inch length of 2½-inch-
    diameter post
2¾ inches of 3½-inch-diameter
    post
Gesso
⅓ yard of black felt
6x6-inch piece of ¼-inch birch
    plywood
3½ inches of ³⁄₁₆-inch dowel
Modeling compound (a clay
    that can be shaped for
    feet and then baked)
Polyester fiberfill
Acrylic paint in the following
    colors: navy, dark red,
    flesh, black, gold, ivory
Matte-finish clear acrylic spray
Small foam brushes
Small artist's brushes for detail
1-inch wire nails
Antiquing medium
Paint thinner
Fine sandpaper
Bandsaw
Drill press
³⁄₁₆-inch drill bit
Glue gun

INSTRUCTIONS
Use the exploded Assembly Diagram, *left*, for visual reference when assembling.

SHOES: Shape modeling compound into two 3-inch ropes approximately ⅜ inch in diameter. Fold each rope in half, leaving ends flared slightly to resemble shoes. Shape as desired, molding the two shoes together into one shape. Before baking, use a ³⁄₁₆-inch dowel to poke a hole completely through the back (heel) of the shoes where they are molded together. *Note:* The dowel for the base will go through the shoes and into the bottom of the doll body. Bake the shoes in an oven at 300 degrees for 20 minutes; cool and set aside.

continued

JACKET: The full-size pattern for the jacket is on page 44.

Use ¼-inch seams for all stitching. Cut jacket from black felt.

With right sides facing, sew one sleeve/arm piece to each piece of jacket front and back, matching AB lines on pattern. With right sides facing, sew assembled jacket front pieces to assembled jacket back pieces, beginning at the shoulder edge (B), stitching around the entire sleeve to the underarm (A), and down the jacket side. Turn and stuff arms. (See the jacket drawing on page 45, *bottom*.)

Coat jacket with gesso, inside and out; dry. (For faster drying, set jacket in sun.) When dry, paint lower 1 inch of arms flesh for hands. Paint ¾-inch red band around wrists. Paint remainder of jacket navy. Let dry thoroughly.

HAT: Cut 3½ inches from one end of 2½-inch-diameter post. Slightly taper on all sides for top of hat shape, referring to the photograph on pages 42 and 43. Drill a ³/₁₆-inch hole 1 inch deep into the center of the bottom of this piece.

Cut a 4¼-inch-diameter circle from ¼-inch plywood for hat brim. Drill a ³/₁₆-inch hole through the center of this piece. Glue a ³/₁₆-inch-diameter dowel that measures 1³/₁₆ inches long into the top of the hat and through the brim to connect the two pieces. (End of dowel will insert into head.) Set aside.

BODY: Taper the lower 8¾ inches of the remaining 2½-inch-diameter post. The resulting shape is rectangular, with the bottom approximately 1 inch from side to side, and ½ inch from front to back. (See Assembly Diagram on page 45.)

Drill ³/₁₆-inch hole in bottom of post and center of top. Using a scrap piece of post, shape a nose. Glue the nose to the face.

For the base, split lengthwise the 3½-inch piece of post to form a half circle. Drill a ³/₁₆-inch hole in center top of the base. Sand all wood pieces, softening square corners of body.

Painting the pieces

Using acrylic paints, paint top of hat and body ivory. Paint head and nose flesh. Paint base and dowel dark red and hat brim navy. Paint shoes black.

Sand body, hat, hat brim, and base. Brush antiquing medium on all pieces, except shoes and dowel. Antique the jacket also. Let set for a few minutes and wipe off excess. Let all pieces dry.

Paint gold stars as desired on jacket. Paint navy stripes on pants. Paint the vest red. (The vest is shaded in the diagram on page 45.)

Paint black eyes, ivory eyebrows, and mix dark red and ivory to dab on cheek color. Paint dark red stripes on hat. Paint a navy hat band. Paint gold stars on the navy hat band. Paint gold stars and ivory dots on the base as desired.

Turn under neck edge of jacket and nail jacket to body.

Put a 2⅜-inch piece of ³/₁₆-inch dowel through shoes and into legs. Put the other end of the dowel into the base.

Insert dowel on hat brim into top of head.

Spray entire doll, including the jacket, with matte spray finish.

Glue hair, beard, and moustache in place. *Note:* Curly wool may be ordered from All Cooped Up, 560 S. State, No. B1, Orem, UT 84058.

Lady Liberty

Shown on page 42.

Finished height is 16½ inches.

MATERIALS
1 5¾x4-inch cotton flag
Instant tea (for dying flag)
Scraps of ¹/₁₆-inch wire
15¼ inches of 2½-inch-diameter post
Scraps of ¼-inch birch plywood
7 inches of 1x4-inch lumber
4 inches of ⅛-inch dowel
¼-inch toy axle 1-inch in length
No. 6 finishing nail
No. 12x2½-inch flathead wood screw
Acrylic paint in the following colors: dark red, ivory, brown-black, flesh, gold, and navy
Antiquing medium
Paint thinner
Matte-finish clear acrylic spray
Fine sandpaper
Small foam brushes
Small artist's brushes (detail)
Bandsaw
Drill press
Drill bits as follows: ⅛-inch, ¼-inch, ⁷/₃₂-inch, ⁹/₆₄-inch
Hammer
Glue gun
No. 6 finishing nail

INSTRUCTIONS
Use the exploded Assembly Diagram, *opposite*, for visual reference when assembling.

Mix a strong batch of instant tea and dip flag. Rinse flag in cold water. Let dry; set aside.

Cutting the pieces
BODY: Referring to the diagram, *opposite*, taper the top 5½ to 6 inches of post. The tapered post will resemble a sharpened pencil, with the top point measuring approximately ¾ inches square. Save scrap pieces. Drill a ⁹/₆₄-inch pilot hole in the bottom center of the body.

ARMS: Use scraps from tapering the body to make two arms. Arms should measure approximately 5½ inches long with a diameter of ½ to ¾ inches at the top (shoulder) and coming to a point at the bottom (hand). Use a small knife or sandpaper to taper right arm at shoulder end as desired.

NOSE: Use another scrap left over from tapering the body to slice off a nose piece measuring approximately 1 inch long.

STARS: Cut three stars from birch plywood.

Drill ⅛-inch holes in stars and in the top of the head as shown on diagram, *right.* Note: Angle the holes in the head for stars.

BASE: Cut 1-inch lumber into two squares, one 2⅝ inches, the other 3½ inches. Drill a ⁷⁄₃₂-inch shank hole through the center of base pieces.

Sand all pieces. Body piece will look better if sanded all over to soften and round tapered sides.

Painting the pieces

Paint nose, face, arms, and body with flesh-color acrylic paint. Referring to the diagram, *right,* and the photograph on page 42, paint navy on body beginning 3½ inches from top point and angling to 10 inches from top. Paint lower section ivory. *Note:* Stripes and dots are painted later.

Paint small base piece navy; paint larger base piece red.

Paint stars gold.

Let all pieces dry thoroughly. Sand all pieces.

Brush antiquing medium mixture on all pieces. Let set a few minutes, then wipe off.

Referring to the photograph on page 42, paint eyes and eyebrows black and lips red. Mix dark red and ivory to achieve a lighter rose; dab finger in mixture and pat on cheeks for blush. Dab brown-black around top of post for hair as desired. Paint small toy axle brown-black.

Paint dark red stripes on ivory skirt and randomly dot navy bodice with ivory. Let dry.

Paint ⅛-inch dowel dark red. Let dry; cut into four 1-inch pieces.

Nail arm without flag to body with a No. 6 finishing nail.

Screw one No. 12 wood screw into the bottom of the red base square, through the blue base square, and into the bottom of the body to attach pieces.

Glue the ¼-inch toy axle into the top of the head.

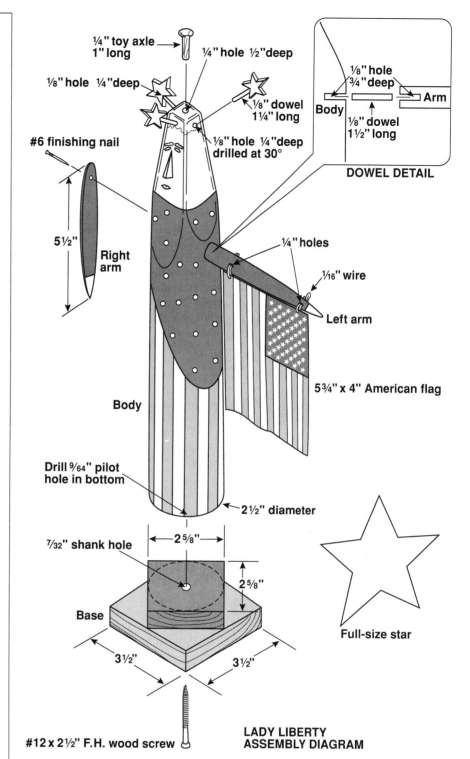

DOWEL DETAIL

LADY LIBERTY ASSEMBLY DIAGRAM

Glue three dowel pieces into stars, then glue them into holes in head. Glue on nose.

Glue ⅛-inch dowel 1½ inches long into second arm piece at shoulder. Drill one small hole 1¼ inches from the point of the arm. Drill a second hole 4½ inches from the point of the arm. Push small pieces of wire through the left side of the flag to line up with the holes in the arm. Stick wire pieces through holes in arm. Twist ends of wire and bend them down to secure.

Put arm dowel into drilled hole in left side of body.

Spray matte-finish acrylic spray over entire doll, including the flag.

PRAIRIE DOLLS

WESTWARD HO

As wagon trains rolled westward and
settlers put down family roots,
cloth dolls were likely a pioneer child's
only toy and most cherished
companion. The friendly faces and
gentle spirit of the dolls in this chapter
recapture those simpler times.

Traveling across the
Geranium Trail, Joshua
and Emma, *right,* pause
for a brief rest. Dressed
for socializing, they are
heading to town to pick
up a few supplies and
visit with old friends.

Finely embroidered
faces give this pioneer
pair quiet sophistica-
tion. Powder blush
provides cheek color
that would have been
natural from long days
in the sun on the open
plains.

Joshua's hair is styled
from fine yarn, and

Emma's locks get curl
by unraveling an old
bouclé sweater.

Simple muslin bodies
are topstitched at the
knees and elbows to
give the dolls the
flexibility to sit or stand
in any setting.

High-button vinyl
shoes and suedelike
boots finish these
delightfully realistic
period costumes.

Patterns for 17-inch
Joshua and 15-inch
Emma begin on page
54. Instructions begin
on page 60.

Personifying the rich heritages of diverse cultures, dolls like the handsome Indian couple, *opposite* and *above,* make fascinating additions to any collection.

Intricate trims and details distinguish the unique costume traditions of Little Dove and White Feather.

Use brushed flannel and suedelike fabric scraps for their clothes. Gather old silver, turquoise jewelry, assorted beads, and small feathers for embellishments.

If you want to showcase the dolls with a teepee similar to the one in the photo, gather tree branches and form a cone-shaped frame.

Tie the top branches with twine to maintain the shape. Cut a circle from chamois or suedelike fabric to fit over the frame. Make a slit to the center. Cut out a small circle in the center that will fit around the top branches. Glue the

fabric to the top branches to hold it in place. Use black acrylic paint and an artist's brush to decorate the teepee with Indian motifs.

Instructions and patterns for the dolls, including faces and clothing, are on pages 54–62.

Enjoying an afternoon on the lawn of their down-scaled saltbox, the miniature colonial doll family, *right,* can be crafted from scrap-bag finds and adapted to resemble your own family members.

Our seven relatives span the generations from baby to grandmother. Using the basic patterns, you can expand your clan by stitching up a houseful of children, aunts, uncles, and country cousins. Outlines are given for the faces that greet you here, but by changing the colors of floss, you can personalize the dolls to resemble your own family members.

These little folks range in size from 2 (Baby Burt) to 6½ inches (the grown-ups).

Instructions begin on page 62, and patterns are on pages 64 and 65.

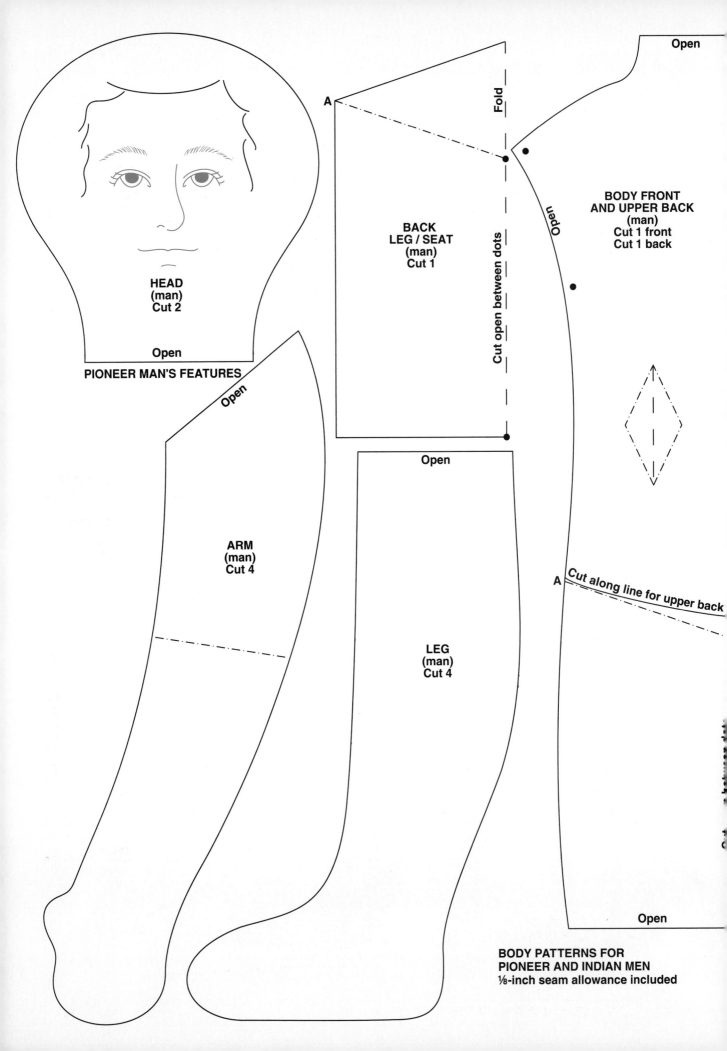

HEAD
(man)
Cut 2

Open

PIONEER MAN'S FEATURES

A

Fold

BACK
LEG / SEAT
(man)
Cut 1

Cut open between dots

Open

Open

**BODY FRONT
AND UPPER BACK**
(man)
Cut 1 front
Cut 1 back

Open

Open

ARM
(man)
Cut 4

LEG
(man)
Cut 4

A   Cut along line for upper back

Open

**BODY PATTERNS FOR
PIONEER AND INDIAN MEN**
⅛-inch seam allowance included

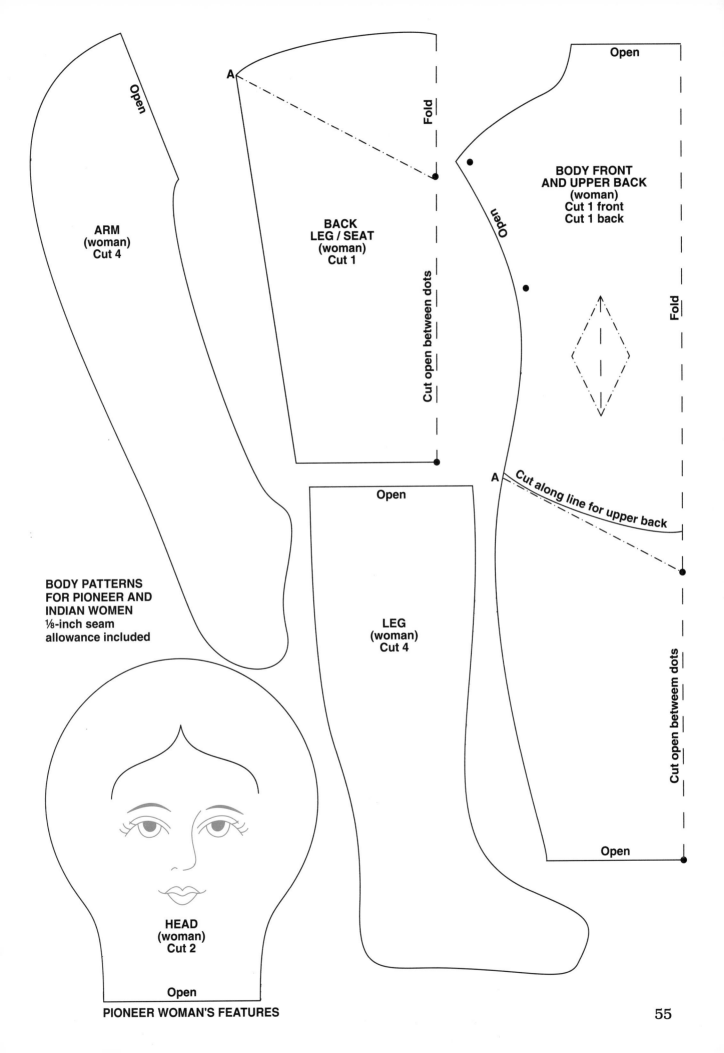

Open

A

Fold

Open

**BODY FRONT
AND UPPER BACK
(woman)
Cut 1 front
Cut 1 back**

Fold

**ARM
(woman)
Cut 4**

**BACK
LEG / SEAT
(woman)
Cut 1**

Cut open between dots

A Cut along line for upper back

Open

**LEG
(woman)
Cut 4**

Cut open betweem dots

**BODY PATTERNS
FOR PIONEER AND
INDIAN WOMEN**
⅛-inch seam
allowance included

Open

**HEAD
(woman)
Cut 2**

Open

PIONEER WOMAN'S FEATURES

55

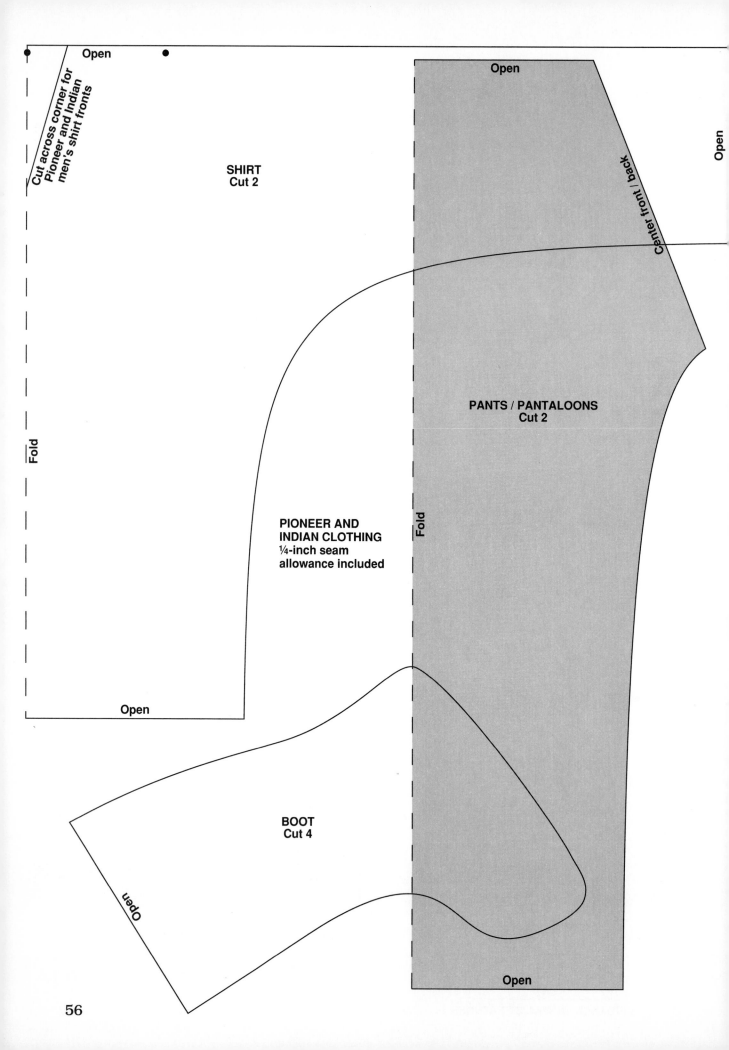

Open

Cut across corner for Pioneer and Indian men's shirt fronts

SHIRT
Cut 2

Open

Fold

PIONEER AND INDIAN CLOTHING
¼-inch seam allowance included

Open

BOOT
Cut 4

Open

Open

Center front / back

Open

PANTS / PANTALOONS
Cut 2

Fold

Open

56

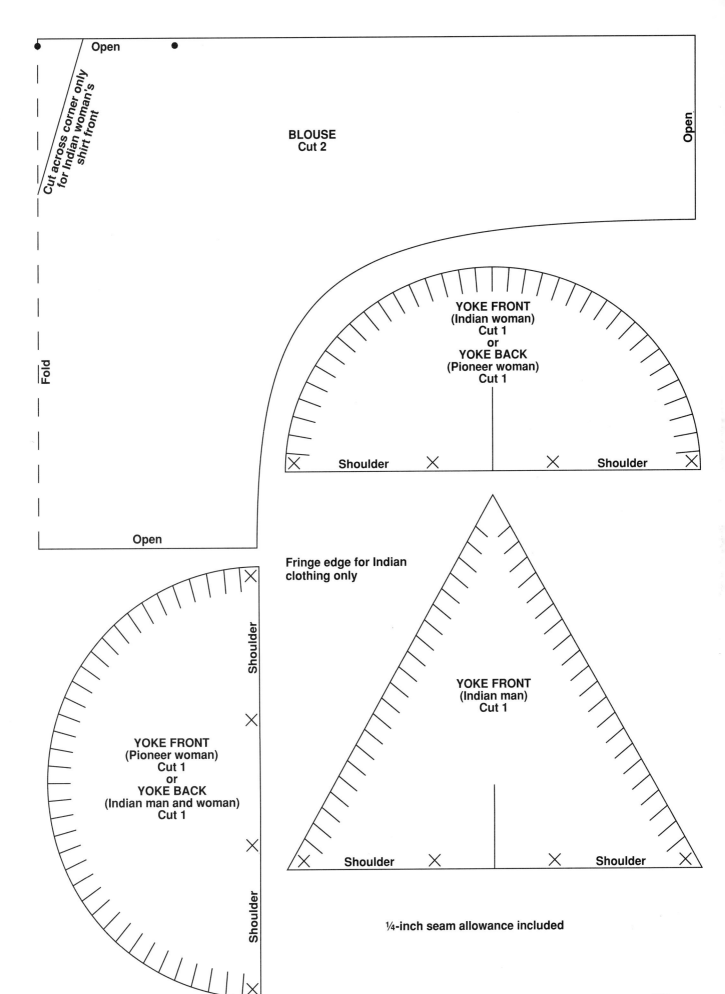

Open

Cut across corner only
for Indian woman's
shirt front

Fold

Open

BLOUSE
Cut 2

Open

YOKE FRONT
(Indian woman)
Cut 1
or
YOKE BACK
(Pioneer woman)
Cut 1

Shoulder ✕ ✕ Shoulder

Fringe edge for Indian
clothing only

✕ Shoulder

✕

YOKE FRONT
(Pioneer woman)
Cut 1
or
YOKE BACK
(Indian man and woman)
Cut 1

✕

Shoulder

✕

YOKE FRONT
(Indian man)
Cut 1

Shoulder ✕ ✕ Shoulder

¼-inch seam allowance included

57

Embroidery Stitches

These diagrams are for the embroidery stitches mentioned in this book. Particular stitches are noted in the how-to instructions for dolls with embroidered faces.

Outline stitch
(also called stem stitch)

Straight stitch

French knot stitch

Satin stitch

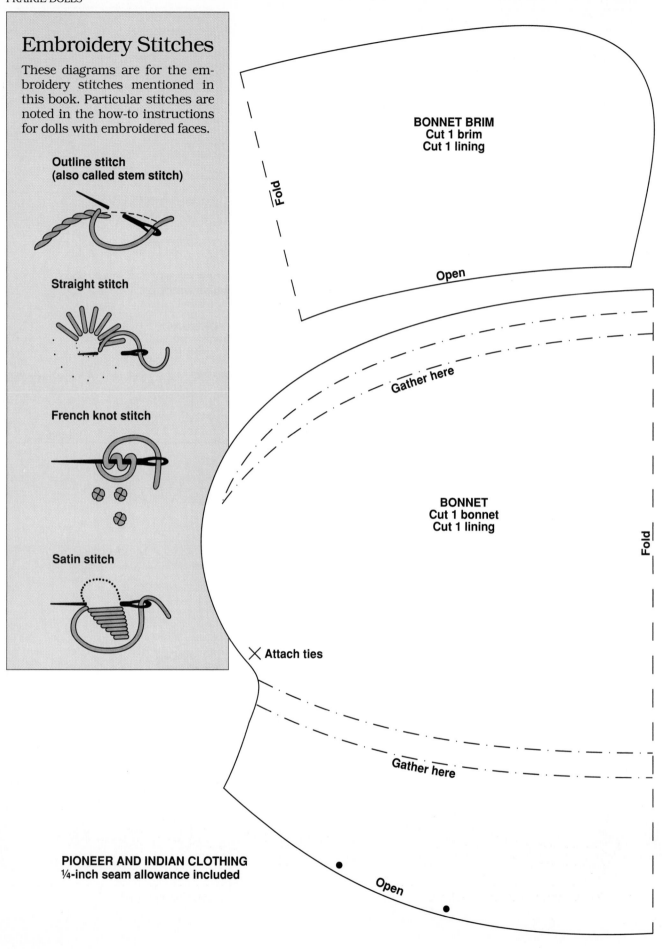

BONNET BRIM
Cut 1 brim
Cut 1 lining

Fold

Open

Gather here

BONNET
Cut 1 bonnet
Cut 1 lining

Fold

✕ **Attach ties**

Gather here

Open

PIONEER AND INDIAN CLOTHING
¼-inch seam allowance included

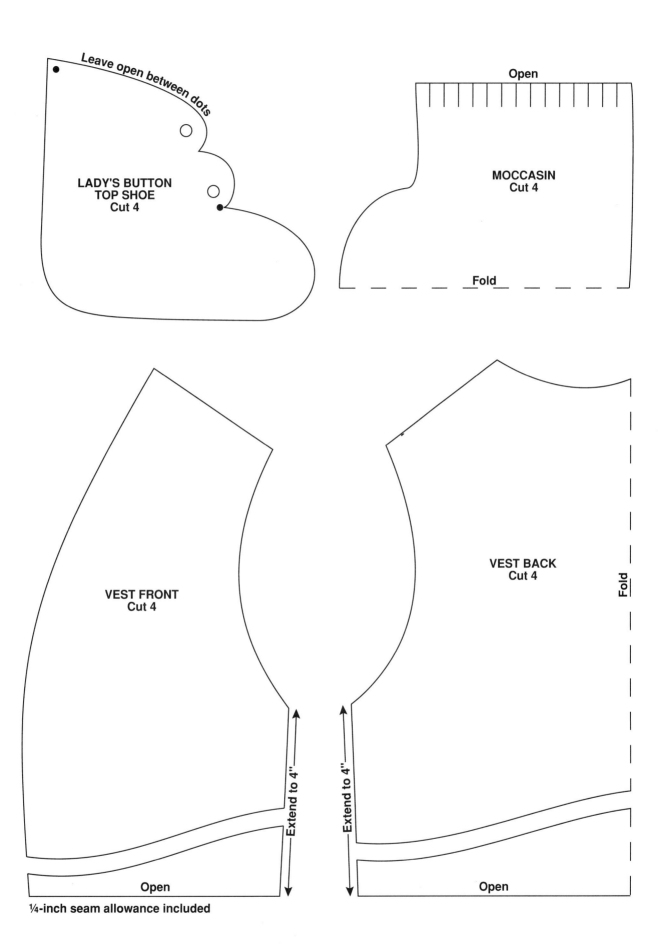

Leave open between dots

LADY'S BUTTON
TOP SHOE
Cut 4

Open

MOCCASIN
Cut 4

Fold

VEST FRONT
Cut 4

VEST BACK
Cut 4

Fold

Extend to 4"

Extend to 4"

Open

Open

¼-inch seam allowance included

Pioneer and Indian Dolls

Shown on pages 48–51.

Dolls are 17 inches (male) and 15 inches (female) tall.

MATERIALS
For pioneer dolls
⅓ yard of muslin (makes two pioneer doll bodies)
Polyester fiberfill
Tracing paper
Dressmaker's carbon
¼-inch-wide elastic
Cardboard

For pioneer woman
Scraps of DMC embroidery floss in the following colors: dark tan (436), black-brown (3371), light blue (3752), coral (760), burgundy (816), and light pink (3713)
Scraps of fabric as follows: gray cotton (bonnet), pink cotton (bonnet lining), floral print cotton (blouse, skirt, and yoke), muslin (petticoat and pantaloons), black cotton (stockings), and gray vinyl (shoes)
⅔ yard of lace edging
Four small gray beads (buttons on shoes)
Light brown bouclé yarn for hair

For pioneer man
Scraps of DMC embroidery floss in the following colors: charcoal (3799), blue gray (927), medium brown (300), dark tan (436), rust (3777), and coral (760)
Scraps of fabric as follows: muslin (shirt), navy cotton (pants), gold brushed flannel (boots), light gold brushed flannel (vest), and plaid (scarf)
Brown brushed acrylic yarn for hair

For Indian dolls
⅓ yard of light brown cotton (makes two Indian doll bodies)
Polyester fiberfill
Tracing paper
Dressmaker's carbon
Beads, feathers, and jewelry
Black brushed acrylic yarn for hair

For Indian woman
Scraps of DMC embroidery floss in the following colors: black-brown (3371), brown (433), rust (3777), dark coral (3328), and white
Scraps of fabric as follows: rust cotton (blouse and yoke), loosely woven rayon in a stripe or print (skirt), and gold brushed flannel (moccasins)
Four small turquoise beads (earrings and buttons on cuffs)

For Indian man
Scraps of DMC embroidery floss in the following colors: black-brown (3371), brown (433), light brown (301), dark brown (938), and ecru
Scraps of fabric as follows: tan brushed flannel (shirt and pants), and gold brushed flannel (moccasins)
¼-inch-wide elastic
5 inches of ⅛-inch-wide leather lacing
Six small feathers

INSTRUCTIONS
For all doll bodies
A ⅛-inch seam allowance is included on each pattern on pages 54 and 55. Use ⅛-inch seams for all stitching on doll bodies.

Solid lines on patterns are cutting lines. Broken lines indicate where a pattern is placed on the fabric fold for cutting. Lines with alternating dots and dashes are stitch lines (darts, special topstitching). Embroidery outlines appear in blue.

Trace patterns onto tracing paper; cut out. For each doll, pin patterns to body fabric and cut out all shapes except the head front. (Face will be embroidered before cutting this piece.)

Mark darts as shown on patterns on wrong sides of fabric pieces. Mark stitching (dot/dash) line on the right side of the back leg/seat fabric piece.

Using dressmaker's carbon, trace facial features onto front of head. Faces for pioneer dolls are on head patterns on pages 54 and 55. Use face patterns at *right* for the Indian dolls.

EMBROIDERING THE FACES: Refer to the stitch diagrams on page 58. Use two strands of floss and outline stitches for all embroidery except women's lips and men's and women's irises and pupils. For these areas, use two strands and satin stitches.

For pioneer woman, use dark tan (436) for nose, eyebrows, and top line of eyelids; black-brown (3371) for edge of eyelids, pupil of eyes, and eyelashes; light blue (3752) for outside of eyes; coral (760) for upper lip; burgundy (816) for line through lips; and light pink (3713) for lower lip.

For pioneer man, use medium brown (300) for eyebrows; dark tan (436) for nose, top line of eyelids, and dimple in chin; charcoal (3799) for edge of eyelids, pupil of eyes, and eyelashes; blue gray (927) for outside of eyes; coral

FEATURES FOR INDIAN MAN AND WOMAN (Head shape, pages 54 and 55)

(760) for upper lip; and rust (3777) for lower lip line.

For Indian woman, use black-brown (3371) for eyebrows, edge of upper eyelids, pupil of eyes, and line around iris; brown (433) for top line of eyelids, iris of eyes, and nose; white to fill in area under iris; dark coral (3328) for upper and lower lips; and rust (3777) for line through lips and under bottom lip.

For Indian man, use black-brown (3371) for eyebrows, bottom edge of eyelids, and iris of eye; brown (433) for top line of eyelids, nose, and chin; light brown (301) for lip; dark brown (938) for outline of lip and line for lower lip; and ecru to fill in eyes below irises and center of pupils.

When all stitching is completed, press fabric on back side and cut out head shape.

ASSEMBLING THE BODY: Sew darts. Clip once at center of dart, being careful not to clip into stitching. Press darts to one side.

With right sides facing, sew leg/seat piece to back of body, matching pieces at A (see patterns). Cut a slit on leg/seat piece between dots marked on pattern.

With right sides facing, sew front and back of body together, leaving leg bottoms, arms, and neck open. Clip curves; turn right side out. Topstitch across the stitching (dot-dash) line on each leg. Stuff body above and below stitched line.

With right sides facing, stitch the arm pieces together and leg pieces together, leaving straight ends open for turning. Clip all curves. Turn each piece right side out and stuff. If arm and leg bending is desired, leave a ¼-inch-wide space unstuffed at the knees (where leg joins body) and elbows (dot/dash line); topstitch across these unstuffed areas.

Baste the leg and arm openings closed. Be sure to align the leg seams at the center back to make the toes point forward when the legs are joined to the body.

With right sides facing, sew the head back and front together, leaving neck open. Clip curves. Turn the head right side out and stuff. To strengthen the neck, insert a cotton swab into the head

stuffing, leaving half of it exposed to insert into the body.

Insert neck of head into body neck opening. Fold body neck opening ¼ inch inward; whipstitch head in place.

Sew arms to body in same manner, folding ½ inch of body fabric to inside before stitching arms in place. *Note:* Shoulder curve of arm should be well inside body before stitching. The thumb should strike 1½ inches below stitching at top of thigh.

Whipstitch legs to assembled body. Be sure to align seams of each leg with center of leg opening on body and to have toes pointing forward.

HAIR: For pioneer man and both Indians, use a soft yarn such as brushed acrylic. Yarn for pioneer woman's hair should be a fine, loopy bouclé. (We unraveled an old sweater to get the curly look.)

For the pioneer woman, Indian woman, and Indian man, loop yarn 24 times around a 15-inch width of cardboard. Remove yarn from cardboard. Spread bundle to about 3 inches wide. Use a sewing machine to stitch across center.

Hand-stitch yarn to the doll's head at center stitch line (hair part) and again about 2½ inches on either side of the center part. Trim hair to an even length.

Pull five strands of yarn from the crown of the Indian man's head. Twist the five strands and the 5-inch length of leather lacing together. Wrap the yarn and lacing around in a bun-shape and stitch to the crown with thread. (See the photograph on page 50.) Braid the remaining yarn into one long braid. Tack two feathers at the bottom of the bun.

Make two braids for the Indian woman. Leave yarn loose for the pioneer woman.

Follow directions above for the pioneer man, using 7-inch-wide cardboard. Stitch the part slightly off center. Sew yarn to doll's head with part on the right. Shape hair to head; trim and tack in place.

For the clothing

A ¼-inch seam allowance is included on each pattern on pages 56–59. Use ¼-inch seams for the stitching on all clothing.

WOMAN'S BLOUSE OR MAN'S SHIRT: Trace blouse, shirt, and yoke patterns on pages 56 and 57 onto tracing paper; cut out. Cut these pieces from designated fabrics. *Note:* Mark yokes so you will know which piece to use for each doll. Do not fringe the edges of the pioneer woman's yoke.

With right sides facing, sew the shirt front and back together at shoulders, leaving an opening between dots. Turn to right side, and cut center front to dot. Press.

Make a 1-inch slit at the center of the yoke front for the Indian woman and at the center of the yoke back for the pioneer woman to allow the yoke to slip over their heads. Make a 1-inch slit at the front of the Indian man's yoke.

With right sides facing, sew the yoke front and back together between the X markings on shoulder (see pattern); press.

For the pioneer woman, cut a 2x21-inch strip of blouse fabric. Sew short edges together, right sides facing; press, turn right side out. Fold strip in half lengthwise. Gather strip to fit around edge of blouse yoke. Lay ruffle against right side of yoke with raw edges of ruffle and curved edge of yoke together; machine-stitch. Turn ruffle down in place and press.

With wrong sides facing, sew yoke to blouse at neckline and around slit opening. Clip corners and curves; turn and press. Topstitch pioneer woman's yoke to blouse along gathered edge. Sew arm and side seams. Hem sleeves to fit arms of doll; hem bottom of shirt or blouse.

Add row of beads above the yoke fringe for the Indian man. Cut ½-inch slits around Indian yokes to fringe edges.

VEST (for pioneer man): Trace the vest front and back patterns (page 59), extending the sides to 4 inches. Cut pieces from flannel. With right sides facing, sew sides of fronts to backs in sets. One set will be the lining. With right sides facing, sew the two vest sets together along the front edges and the sleeves, leaving the bottom and shoulder edges free. Turn vest right side out. Hand-stitch front and back shoulder seams *continued* together. Cut a fringe along bottom edge. Topstitch ¼ inch above fringe.

SCARF (for pioneer man): To make a pattern for a scarf, draw an 11-inch line on paper. Measure up from center of 11-inch line and mark a point 5½ inches above center. Draw a line from that point to end of 11-inch line on both sides to form a triangle. Cut triangle pattern from plaid scarf fabric and tie at neckline of the pioneer man.

PANTS (for both male dolls): Trace pattern on page 56 onto tissue paper; cut out. Cut pioneer man's pants from navy fabric. Cut Indian man's pants from brushed flannel.

Fringe is added to Indian man's pants before assembly. Cut a strip of flannel 1½ inches wide and 9 inches in length. Fringe one long edge. With right sides of fabric facing and fringe toward front of leg, place the unclipped edge along fold line of each leg, beginning ½ inch down from top (waist). Machine-stitch ¼ inch in from unclipped edge of fabric strip. Fold fringe back and topstitch in place.

With right sides facing, sew center front and center back seams; sew leg seams. Press waistband ½ inch to inside, leaving a small space open at back for threading elastic. Insert 5 inches of elastic through waistband. Sew ends of elastic together; stitch waistband opening closed. Sew a ¼-inch hem in bottom of pant legs; press.

SKIRT (for both female dolls): Cut one 6½x1½-inch strip of skirt fabric for waistband. Turn long edges in ¼ inch on both sides; press. Fold strip in half lengthwise; press. Refold waistband in half with right sides facing and stitch across short ends. Turn right side out. Press ends flat.

Cut one 24x8-inch rectangle from skirt fabric. With right sides facing, sew 8-inch sides together, leaving 2 inches open at top. Press seam open. Gather to fit waistband.

Position waistband over gathering; topstitch band onto skirt.

Turn hem of skirt under ⅛ inch, then ½ inch; press and stitch.

PANTALOONS (for pioneer woman): Use pants pattern on page 56 and instructions for man's pants, *left*, to make muslin pantaloons. Shorten to desired length; hem. Stitch elastic at bottom of each pant leg to fit doll's leg.

STOCKINGS (for pioneer woman): Using the woman's leg pattern on page 55 for stockings, cut four from black cotton. With right sides facing, sew together in sets, leaving the top open. Place stockings on doll's legs, turn under raw edge, and hand-stitch to legs at the tops of the stockings.

PETTICOAT (for pioneer woman): Cut a 15x9½-inch rectangle from muslin. With right sides facing, sew 9½-inch sides together. Fold top down ½ inch and stitch to make a casing for waistline, leaving a small opening for inserting elastic. Thread 3½ inches of elastic through the casing; sew the ends of the elastic together. Hem the bottom of the petticoat and stitch lace at bottom, if desired. Turn right side out.

BONNET (for pioneer woman): Trace patterns on page 58 onto tracing paper; cut out. Cut from bonnet fabrics.

With right sides facing, sew bonnet to bonnet lining. Leave a small opening between dots at bottom for turning. Turn bonnet right side out and topstitch bottom of bonnet approximately ⅛ inch in from edge.

With right sides facing, stitch brim to brim lining, leaving inside edge open as marked on pattern. Turn right side out. Fold raw edges inward ¼ inch; press. Topstitch ⅛ inch in from outside edge of brim, leaving inside edge open. Cut a piece of cardboard that will fit inside the brim, leaving ⅛ inch clear along open edge of brim. Insert cardboard and stitch opening closed.

Gather front of bonnet ½ inch in from edge to fit along inside edge of brim. Lay atop brim and stitch bonnet to brim along gathering line. Gather back of bonnet 1 inch from bottom edge tight

enough to fit nicely around base of doll's head.

Cut two strips of fabric 1x7 inches. Fold each strip in half lengthwise, right sides facing, and stitch along long edge. Turn right side out and press. Cut one end of each tie at an angle. Hand-stitch other end to bonnet for ties.

MOCCASINS, SHOES, AND BOOTS: *For Indian man and woman*, trace moccasin pattern on page 59 onto tissue paper; cut out. Cut moccasins from flannel; fringe tops. Refold each piece of moccasin fabric with right sides facing. Stitch front and back seams of each. Leave tops open. Turn to right sides. Fold fringed tops down; hand-stitch down at back and front to secure.

For pioneer woman, trace shoe pattern from 59 onto tissue paper; cut out. Cut shoes from gray vinyl. Refold each piece of shoe fabric with right sides facing. Stitch backs, bottoms, and toes of shoes. Leave openings between the dots marked on the pattern. Clip curves. Turn right sides out. Sew small beads to the inside flap of each shoe according to pattern markings. Slip shoes on doll's feet, overlapping top flaps. Sew flaps together behind beads.

For pioneer man, trace boot pattern on page 56 onto tissue paper; cut out. Cut boots from brushed flannel. With right sides facing, sew around boots, leaving top open. Turn; hem top edges.

TO FINISH: Decorate Indian dolls with beads, feathers, and jewelry.

Doll House Family

Shown on pages 52 and 53.

Dolls range in height from 2 to 6½ inches.

MATERIALS
For all seven dolls
½ yard of muslin
Matching thread
Scraps of embroidery floss in desired colors for faces and hair

Pink powder blush
Polyester fiberfill
Cardboard squares
    (2 and 3½ inches)
Solid, check, and print fabric
    scraps for clothing
Brown and black fabric for boots
Lace and ribbon scraps
¼ yard of 4-inch wide eyelet lace
Matching thread
Narrow round cord elastic
Small buttons
Tracing paper
Dressmaker's carbon

INSTRUCTIONS
Cutting the patterns
Add ¼-inch seam allowances to *all* patterns before cutting. Use ¼-inch seams on all stitching.

Solid lines on patterns are cutting lines; broken lines indicate where a pattern piece is placed on the fold for cutting. Embroidery stitch outlines appear in blue.

Trace patterns on pages 64 and 65 onto tracing paper; cut out all patterns. Lay adult and child body, leg, and arm patterns, and baby body pattern on muslin and trace around edges. Do not cut any body pieces until facial embroidery is completed. Trace facial features from page 64 onto heads using dressmaker's carbon. Or, change the features to resemble your family members.

Using one strand of floss in colors desired, embroider facial features. Add blush to cheeks of females and baby.

Cut all remaining body pieces from muslin.

For baby
BODY: With right sides facing, pin front and back together. Sew, leaving openings at bottom between dots marked on pattern. Clip curves; turn and press.

HAIR: Using one strand of floss, pull individual strands through fabric on head; knot to the inside. Cut strands to ¼ inch. Stuff body; stitch opening closed.

CLOTHING: Adding ¼-inch seams, trace patterns for baby suit front and baby suit back on page 65 onto tracing paper. Fold a fabric scrap, right sides facing, so that the selvage edges are on top of one another. For back, place

back center of pattern atop the selvages; cut out. For front, place center on fold; cut out.

Sew center back seam from bottom to dot; press open. Place front atop back with right sides facing. Sew shoulder seams. Hand-turn neck and armhole edges under and blindstitch. Sew side seams; sew crotch seam. By hand, turn under leg edges and blindstitch. Place suit on doll. Tack back seam closed. Hand-sew a scrap of lace to neck edge.

For woman and girl
BODY: Use adult body patterns for mother and grandmother; use child body patterns for girl. With right sides facing, pin body front and back together. Sew, leaving bottom open for legs and leaving arm openings between the dots marked on the pattern; clip curves and turn. Turn armhole and bottom edges under; press.

With right sides facing, pin arm pieces together in sets. Sew, leaving the tops open; clip curves. Turn and press. Stuff each arm firmly to stitching (dot/dash) line (elbow). Stitch across dot/dash lines. Stuff tops of arms lightly.

Sew the legs together in sets following the directions for arms.

Insert arms into openings on body. Machine-stitch arm openings closed, securing arms. Stuff body firmly. Insert legs into bottom. Stitch across bottom to close. (*Note:* Height of doll may be adjusted by inserting less or more of the legs into the opening.)

HAIR: Wrap all six strands of floss approximately 10 times around the 3½-inch cardboard square. Carefully remove and tack center to part line of head with one strand of same color floss. Clip loops; separate strands with needle or fine comb. Trim and shape hair to desired length and hairstyle.

CLOTHING: Adding ¼-inch seams, trace patterns for skirt, woman's blouse/top, girl's top, adult boot, and child boot on page 65 onto tracing paper.

To cut blouse/top back, fold fabric, right sides facing, with selvage atop selvage. Place center back along selvage; cut out. For

front, place center on fold; cut out. Sew center back seam from bottom to dot. Turn up hem on fronts and back; stitch. Hem sleeves.

With right sides facing, sew front and back together at shoulder/sleeve seam and underarm/side seam. Clip to stitching at underarm. Turn under neck edge and blindstitch, clipping if necessary. Press.

Put blouse/top on doll. Blindstitch back opening closed. Hand-sew lace at neck for collar.

Cut skirt from scrap fabric. With right sides facing, sew front to back at one side. Fold under hem and stitch. Turn down ¼ inch at top over round elastic. Tighten to approximately 2 inches; secure ends of elastic. Sew remaining side seam.

For woman's apron, cut a 2½x4½-inch rectangle from wide eyelet lace. Hem one long and two short edges. Fold raw edge of top to inside and gather to 2 inches. Sew to narrow ribbon. Tie around waist. For girl's apron, cut lace design as desired, wrap around waist, and tack in back.

For girl's hat, cut a round piece of lace and tack to head.

For woman's shawl, cut a 1½x4¾-inch rectangle from loosely woven fabric. Pull fabric threads to fringe one long side and both short ends. Put over doll's shoulders; tack in place.

Cut boots from black or brown fabric. Turn tops down inside ¼ inch and stitch. With right sides facing, sew around sides and bottoms. Stuff feet into boots.

For man and boy
BODY: Assemble bodies following directions for woman, *above.*

HAIR: Wrap all six strands of floss approximately 10 times around the 2-inch cardboard square. Carefully remove and tack center to part line of head with one strand of same color floss. Clip loops; separate strands with needle or fine comb. Tack randomly on head with one strand of matching floss; trim.

CLOTHING: Adding ¼-inch seams, trace patterns for man's
continued

shirt, boy's shirt, collar, trousers, adult boot, and child boot, *opposite,* onto tracing paper.

To cut shirt back, place broken line of pattern on fold; cut out. To cut shirt front, fold fabric with right sides facing so one selvage is atop the other. Place pattern center on selvage; cut out. Turn up bottom hem on back and fronts; stitch. Turn front edges in ¼ inch; stitch. With right sides facing, sew fronts to back at shoulders. Hem sleeves. With right sides facing, sew collar together along short ends and outside curve; turn. Press collar. With right sides facing, sew collar to neck edge. Hand-stitch raw edges at neckline to inside of shirt so that the collar lies flat. Sew underarm/side seams with right sides facing. Clip underarm to stitching. Put shirt on doll and blindstitch front closed. Add a small bow tie, if desired.

Hem bottom and top of each trouser piece. Fold each leg, with right sides together; stitch inner leg seam. Turn one leg right side out and place inside other leg. Sew crotch seam. Fold and tack small pleat on each side of center front seam. Place on doll and add buttons and ribbon suspenders.

Cut boots from black cotton fabric. Turn tops down inside ¼ inch and stitch. Sew around sides and bottoms with right sides facing. Stuff feet into boots.

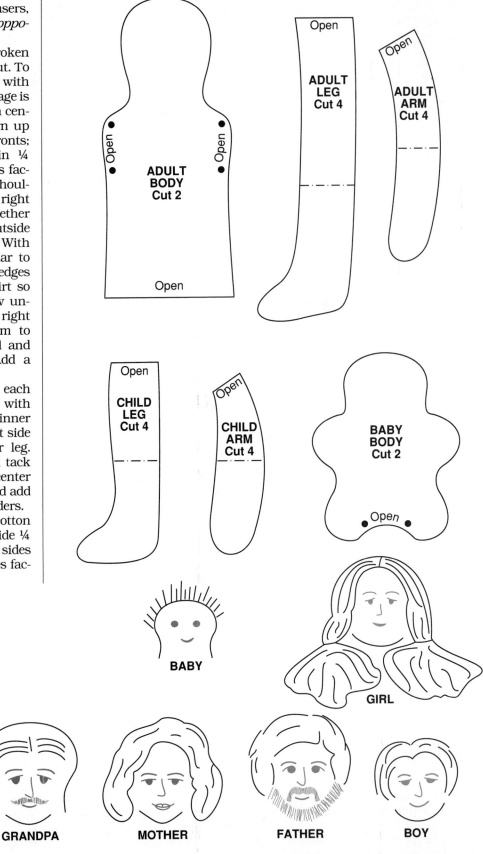

DOLL HOUSE FAMILY

Add ¼-inch seam allowance

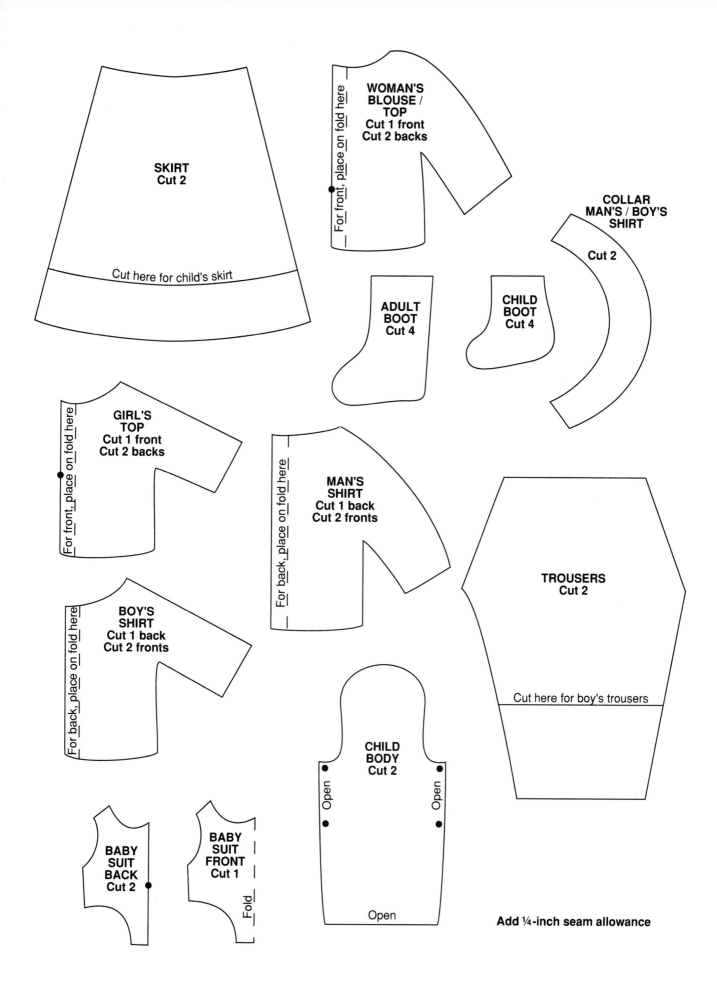

SKIRT
Cut 2

Cut here for child's skirt

WOMAN'S BLOUSE / TOP
Cut 1 front
Cut 2 backs

For front, place on fold here

COLLAR MAN'S / BOY'S SHIRT
Cut 2

ADULT BOOT
Cut 4

CHILD BOOT
Cut 4

GIRL'S TOP
Cut 1 front
Cut 2 backs

For front, place on fold here

MAN'S SHIRT
Cut 1 back
Cut 2 fronts

For back, place on fold here

TROUSERS
Cut 2

Cut here for boy's trousers

BOY'S SHIRT
Cut 1 back
Cut 2 fronts

For back, place on fold here

CHILD BODY
Cut 2

Open

Open

Open

BABY SUIT BACK
Cut 2

BABY SUIT FRONT
Cut 1

Fold

Add ¼-inch seam allowance

SCRAP-BAG DOLLS

FOR CHILDREN

It is through a child's vivid imagination and breathless anticipation that we enjoy and appreciate special occasions. The dolls in this chapter are created with that in mind. Made of soft and supple materials, this gathering of stitched, knitted, and crocheted country playmates will be a joy to craft and give to even the youngest in your family.

Quilting bees always have been a time of fun and friendship. Today's get-together is no exception for Twila, Pearl, and their friend, Francene, *right.*

Always a hit at any social is Pearl's rum cake, served with a piping hot cup of cinnamon tea.

These dolls are an excellent way to use up scraps. Crocheted trims and embroidered doilies from Grandma's attic are fashioned into aprons, collars, and underskirts to accent their soft floral dresses. Strands of yarn are shaped into braids and soft curls and tied with satin ribbons. Faces are painted on with soft acrylics or permanent markers.

Patterns and instructions for these 19-inch calico dolls begin on page 71.

Knitted and crocheted dolls always are favorites of young folks because they are so soft and gentle to squeeze.

Nicolaus and Nancy, *above*, are knitted from shades of heather sport-weight wool yarn on Size 3 needles. The instructions for both dolls are the same—only the colors change.

Their friend Emily, *opposite*, is crocheted from cotton thread with a Size 7 hook. Machine-stitching across the elbow and knee areas gives her the flexibility of a jointed doll.

Her dress and apron are handmade, but her shoes and wig were purchased from a local doll shop.

Instructions for the knitted dolls are on page 70. Instructions for the crocheted doll and information for ordering the wig and shoes are on pages 76 and 77.

Knitted Boy and Girl

Shown on page 69.

Finished height of each doll is 11½ inches.

MATERIALS
Brunswick Pomfret sport-weight yarn: One skein *each* of ecru (5000), camel (535), granite heather (599), teal heather (581), cranberry (557), and berber brown heather (568)
Polyester fiberfill
Size 3 single-pointed knitting needles
Small stitch holder
Tapestry needle
Sewing needle
Scissors
Two ¼-inch charcoal gray buttons for each doll for eyes
10 small stitch markers for the girl's skirt

Gauge: 6 sts in stockinette st = 1 inch; 9 rows = 1 inch
Abbreviations: See page 72.

Note: The instructions for the boy and girl doll are the same; only the colors vary. The color changes for the girl doll are given in parenthesis ( ).

INSTRUCTIONS
HEAD: Starting at the top with Size 3 needles and ecru (ecru), cast on 11 sts.

K in front and back of all sts across—22 sts.

P 1 row. Inc 1 st in every st across, k 1 row—44 sts.

Work even in st st, starting and ending with a p row for 25 rows.

K 2 tog across—22 sts.

P 1 row. Cut ecru.

SHIRT: Join granite heather (camel) and k 3, (inc in next st) 5 times; k 6, (inc in next st) 5 times, k 3—32 sts.

Work even in st st starting and ending with a p row for 15 rows.

Increasing under arms: K 6, (inc in next st) 4 times; k 12, (inc in next st) 4 times, k 6—40 sts.

Work even in st st for 7 more rows. Cut granite heather (do not cut camel).

PANTS: Join teal heather (continue to work in camel). Work 12 rows in st st begining with a k row and ending with a p row.

First leg: K 20 sts, place last 20 sts onto stitch holder. Cast on 2 sts at the end of the row of sts rem on needle, turn. P 22 sts and cast on 2 sts at the end of row—24 sts. *For girl, cut camel and join ecru at this point.*

Continue to work in st st on 24 sts for *36 rows for boy* or *30 rows for girl.* End with a p row. Cut teal heather (ecru).

Boy's shoe: Join berber brown heather and work 6 rows in st st. K 2 tog across—12 sts. P 1 row.

K 2 tog across—6 sts. Cut yarn, leaving 8 inches. With yarn end, gather together the rem sts on the needle and sew shoe together.

Girl's sock and shoe: Join camel and work 6 rows in st st. Cut camel and join berber brown heather. Work shoe as for boy's shoe, *above.*

Second leg: Place sts from holder onto needle and k across. Cast on 2 sts at the end of the row. P 22, cast on 2 sts at the end of the row. Make a second leg to match the first.

ARMS (make 2): With granite heather (camel) cast on 5 sts. K in front and in back of all sts across—10 sts. P 1 row. Inc 1 st in every st across, k 1 row—20 sts. Work even in st st starting and ending with a p row for 31 rows. Cut yarn.

MITTENS: Join cranberry (teal) and work in st st for 6 rows. K 2 tog across—10 sts. P 1 row. K 2 tog across. Cut yarn; gather and sew seams of mitten portion of the arm.

SCARF: With cranberry (teal), cast on 60 sts. K 3 rows. Bind-off. Tie small cranberry (teal) yarn tassels on the ends of the scarf.

HAT: With cranberry (teal), cast on 46 sts. Work in k 1, p 1 ribbing for 3 rows.

Work in st st for 16 rows beginning with a k row and ending with a p row.

K 2 tog across—23 sts. P 1 row.

K 2 tog across except for the last st—12 sts. P 1 row.

K 2 tog across—6 sts. Cut yarn, leaving a 10-inch length. With yarn end, gather together the sts remaining on the needle and sew the back head seam. Stitch a ¾-inch cranberry (teal) pom-pom to the top of the hat.

To make a pom-pom
Wind cranberry (teal) yarn around a 1-inch-wide strip of cardboard 25 times. Remove the yarn from the cardboard strip and tie a double strand of yarn around the center of the bundle. Clip the loops.

SKIRT: With cranberry, cast on 40 sts. Work in k 1, p 1 ribbing for 2 rows. P 1 row.

Marker row: K 4, * place st marker on needle, inc 2, place st marker on needle, k 8, rep from * 4 more times ending with k 4 instead of k 8.

Increasing rows: P 1 row. K 1 row, inc 1 st at both the beg and end of the sts between each set of markers (you will be inc 10 sts on every k row).

Rep the two inc rows until you have 8 sts between each set of markers. P 1 row, removing st markers as you work. Cut cranberry yarn.

For garter st stripes, k 2 rows with each of the following colors: granite heather, camel, granite heather, teal heather, granite heather, camel, granite heather. Cut and weave in all yarn colors.

Join cranberry, k 1 row. P 1 row. K 2 rows. Bind-off in k st. Sew center back skirt seam. Cut a length of cranberry yarn 24 inches long. Double and weave it through the bottom row of the waist ribbing, starting and ending at the back of the skirt. Place skirt on doll and tie a bow with waist yarn strands.

Assembly of dolls
With matching yarn, sew the inside seam of each leg. Sew the back seam of the pants. Stuff the legs of the doll with fiberfill. Beginning at the neck, sew the body back seams. Stuff the body. Beginning at the top of the head, sew half the head seam. Stuff the head. Sew the remaining seam, stuffing the head as necessary. Weave a strand of ecru yarn around the last row of the head and slightly pull on the strand to shape the neck. Knot the strand to secure; weave in the ends.

With granite heather (camel), sew the arm seams together, stuffing arms as you sew. With double strand of cranberry (teal heather), wrap yarn around wrist along top edges of the mittens and tie in knot. Weave in yarn ends. Place completed arms at the shoulders of doll and stitch into place with matching yarn.

FINISHING: Stitch charcoal gray buttons to the doll's face for eyes. Tie the cranberry scarf around the boy's neck and place the cranberry hat on his head. Stitch hat and scarf in place, if desired.

For braids on the girl doll, cut nine 40-inch lengths of berber brown yarn. Place the yarn lengths together and fold them in half. Cut through fold. Tie a piece of cranberry yarn in a bow 1 inch from one end. Divide yarn into three sections of six strands each. From the bow, braid the entire length of yarn to within 1 inch of the other end; tie a second bow of cranberrry yarn. Attach the center of the braid to the top of the doll's head.

With berber brown heather yarn, use the outline stitch shown on page 58 to embroider a small arch at the top of each shoe to form shoe straps. Tie the teal scarf around her neck and place the teal hat on her head over the braids. Stitch hat and scarf in place, if desired.

Calico Dolls

Shown on pages 66 and 67.

Finished height of each doll is 19 inches.

MATERIALS
For one doll
Tracing paper
Graph paper
⅓ yard of muslin for body
1 yard of print fabric for dress and bonnet
14 inches of print fabric for bloomers
27 inches of lace (optional for sleeve and bonnet trim)
1⅓ yard of lace (optional for bottom of skirt)
5 inches of ½-inch elastic for waist of bloomers
5 inches of ¼-inch elastic for sleeves and legs of bloomers
Two ⅜-inch black buttons for shoes
Old doily or dresser scarves for collars and aprons
Yarn for hair
Black acrylic paint for shoes
Acrylic paint or permanent markers in red, blue, and brown for facial features
Pink powder blush

INSTRUCTIONS
Note: Patterns include ¼-inch seam allowances. Sew all seams with right sides facing.

Patterns on pages 74 and 75 are full size. Enlarge the bloomer pattern on page 73 onto graph paper to make a full-size pattern.

For the head/body pattern, align the AB markings of the piece on page 74 with the piece on page 75 to make one complete pattern. For the leg pattern, extend the pattern piece between the broken lines so the leg measures 9 inches from the ankle to the top.

Transfer all pattern pieces to tracing paper. Cut out pieces. Trace around patterns onto fabrics. Cut out all pieces except the front head/body piece.

Referring to the photograph on pages 66 and 67, draw a face onto the head shape. Using acrylic paints or markers, paint the mouth red, the eyes blue, and the nose, freckles, eyelashes, and around the eyes brown. Brush pink powder blusher onto cheeks. Cut out painted head/body piece.

To assemble the doll
BODY: With right sides facing, sew head/body pieces together, beginning at one shoulder and sewing around the head to the other shoulder. Clip at neck curve. Turn right side out.

Stitch arms, right sides facing, to body, matching folds of arm pieces to shoulder seams. Turn body wrong side out. With right sides facing, sew side body seams, underarms, and down around the hands. Clip at underarms. Leave bottom of body open. Turn and stuff arms half way up (elbow); stitch across arms just above stuffing so that the arm bends easily. Stuff arm 1 inch more and sew again above that stuffing. Stitch arm closed where the arm joins body so stuffing from body will not slip into the top of the unstuffed arm.

Stuff the body and head firmly.

Fold each leg piece in half, right sides facing. Stitch each leg together, starting at the top of the leg and continuing around the foot. Turn right side out; firmly stuff each leg half way up (knee). With the toe pointing forward and the seam down the front of the leg, stitch across each leg right above the stuffing. Finish lightly stuffing to within 1 inch of the top of each leg. Baste legs in place at bottom of body. Stitch bottom opening closed.

To make the clothing
SHOES: Using black acrylic paint and the shaded portion of the pattern on page 74 as a guide, paint shoes on feet. Stitch one button on each painted shoe.

DRESS: Cut all pieces from cotton print fabrics. Cut one 11x40-inch rectangle for the skirt.
continued

With right sides facing, sew the bodice fronts to bodice back pieces in sets at shoulder seams. With right sides facing, sew bodice pieces together around neckline and down center back seams. Clip curves; turn right side out and press. Hand-sew crocheted edging or pregathered lace to the inside edge, or machine-topstitch satin ribbon to the outside edge of the bodice neckline as desired.

SLEEVES: Hem bottom edge of sleeve. (Stitch lace trim to inside of sleeve hem, if desired.) Sew elastic approximately 1¼ inches from hem, stretching as you sew to gather the fabric. Gather the top edge of sleeve. With right sides facing, pin sleeve to armhole, matching center of sleeve with shoulder seam and pushing all gathers to the cap of the sleeve. Sew sleeve to bodice.

With right sides facing, sew underarm of sleeve and bodice side with one continuous seam. Clip and turn right side out; overlap back 1 inch and pin together.

SKIRT: With right sides facing, stitch 11-inch edges of skirt rectangle together. Turn the bottom edge under 1 inch and hem. (Options: Make tucks above the hemline; stitch lace at bottom of skirt, or leave plain. See the photograph on pages 66 and 67 for ideas.)

Gather the top edge of the skirt to fit the bodice. With right sides facing, stitch the skirt to the bottom of the bodice.

BLOOMERS: Turn bottom edge of bloomers up ¼ inch and hem. Sew elastic 1¼ inches above the hem, stretching as you sew to gather the fabric. With right sides facing, sew center fronts of bloomers together; sew center backs together.

Turn down ½ inch at upper edge. Machine-stitch to form a casing, leaving 1½ inches unstitched. Insert 5 inches of ¼-inch elastic through the casing at that opening. Sew the ends of the elastic together. Sew opening in casing closed.

With right sides facing and matching center seams, sew inside leg seams together. Turn right side out and put bloomers on doll.

BONNET: Sew lace to right side of one brim piece along curved edge. With right sides facing, sew the two brim pieces together, leaving the straight edge open for turning. Turn right side out and press. Gather the curved edge of the bonnet crown to fit the brim. Matching centers and with right sides facing, stitch crown to brim. Hem bottom edge and short straight sides of bonnet. Stitch elastic along the back edge of the bonnet between X (attach tie) markings on the pattern. Stretch the elastic as you sew to gather the fabric. Cut two pieces of ribbon, each 6 inches in length; fold one end under and stitch to each side of the bonnet at the X markings. Place bonnet on doll's head and tie under chin.

APRON: The aprons shown on the dolls on pages 66 and 67 are made from old embroidered and crocheted doilies. Doilies that were used on dressers or backs and arms of chairs often have one straight edge and curved shapes on the sides and bottom edge. For crocheted doilies, simply weave a piece of ribbon through the openings and tie around the waist of the doll.

For embroidered doilies, stitch a piece of ribbon across the straight edge of the doily to make a waistband. Leave an additional 6 inches on each side of the doily for a bow that can be tied in back.

COLLAR: The removable collar also is made from an oval doily. Cut a slit from the center of one end to the center of the doily. Cut a circular opening in the center to fit around the doll's neck. Turn the cut edge of the opening under and stitch. Hand-stitch ribbon ties at the back. Place around doll's neck and tie at back.

For hair
SHORT HAIR (page 67, *right*): Wrap yarn around four fingers four times. Remove from fingers.

Tie a short piece of yarn in knot around the middle of the loops of yarn. (You will need a total of 60 knotted loop sets.) Position and stitch knots in all locations to cover the head.

PONYTAILS (page 66): Start by measuring a 16-inch length of yarn; do not cut it from the skein. Place sewing machine foot in middle of the 16-inch length; loop yarn and slide second 16 inches under foot. Continue this pattern, sewing to a total width of 4½ inches. (The stitched line down the center of the yarn loops is the hair part.) Stitch the part to the head from front to lower back.

Pull hair to sides and tie into ponytails. If ponytails do not lie down, tack them to head at underside; tie with ribbon. Add short bangs separately.

BRAIDS (page 67, *left*): Start by measuring a 21-inch length of yarn measured; do not cut it from the skein. Follow directions, *above*, for ponytails. After sewing all lengths of yarn together, cut loops at the ends. Braid to within 1½ inches of the bottom; tie ribbon or yarn bow at each end.

Crocheting Abbreviations

beg	begin(ning)
ch	chain
dc	double crochet
hdc	half double crochet
lp(s)	loop(s)
rep	repeat
rnd	round
sc	single crochet
sk	skip
sl st	slip stitch
st(s)	stitch(es)
*	repeat from * as indicated

Knitting Abbreviations

inc	increase
k	knit
p	purl
rem	remaining
rep	repeat
st(s)	stitch(es)
st st	straight stitch
tog	together
*	repeat from * as indicated

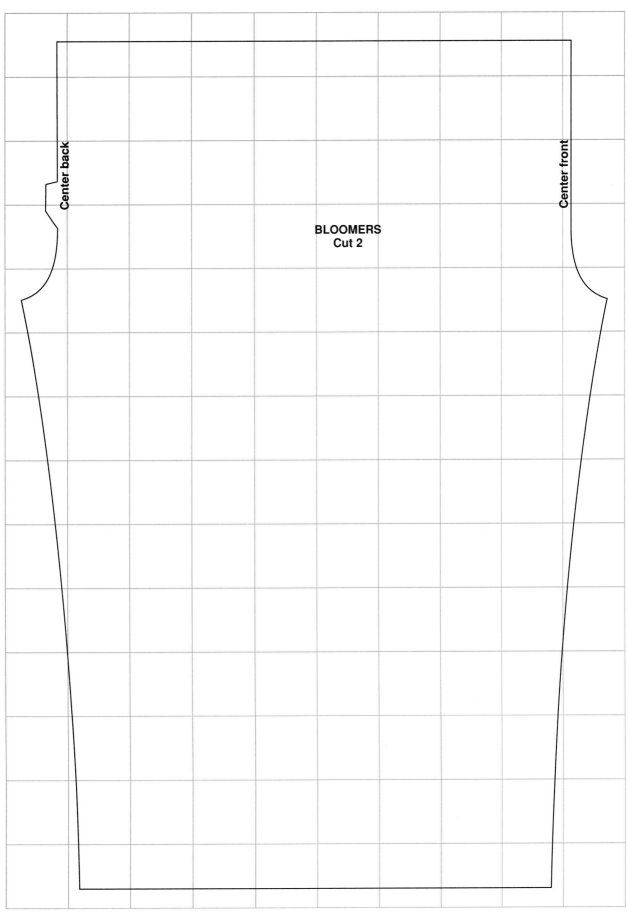

Center back

Center front

BLOOMERS
Cut 2

CALICO DOLLS
¼-inch seam allowance included

1 Square = 1 Inch

73

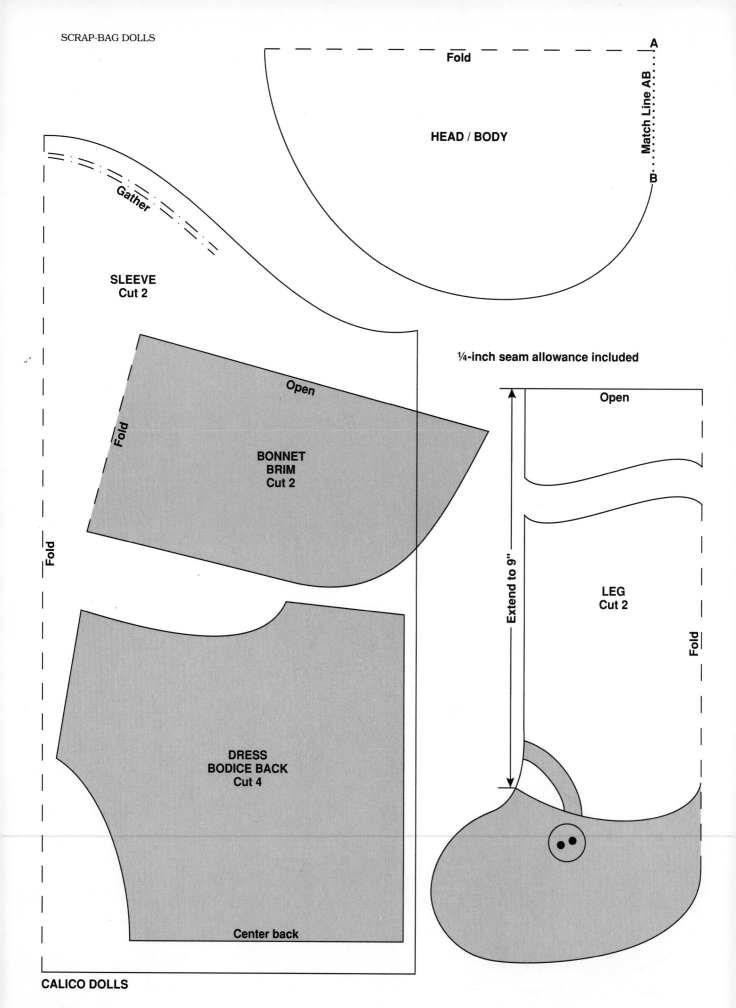

A

Match Line AB

B

Fold

HEAD / BODY

Gather

SLEEVE
Cut 2

¼-inch seam allowance included

Open

Open

Fold

BONNET
BRIM
Cut 2

Extend to 9"

LEG
Cut 2

Fold

Fold

DRESS
BODICE BACK
Cut 4

Center back

CALICO DOLLS

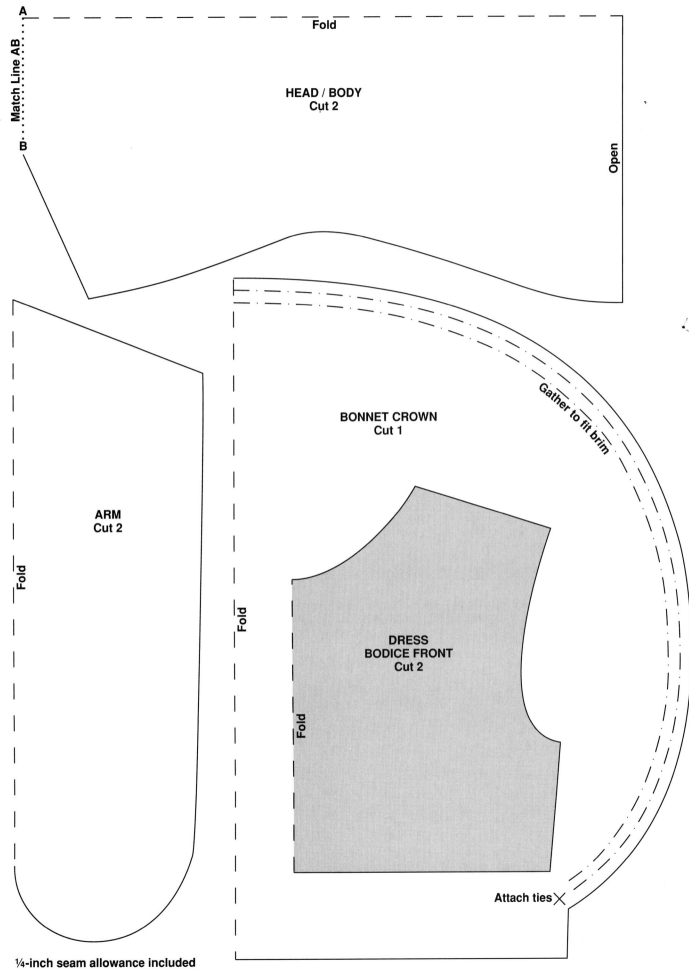

A

Match Line AB

B

Fold

HEAD / BODY
Cut 2

Open

ARM
Cut 2

Fold

BONNET CROWN
Cut 1

Gather to fit brim

Fold

Fold

DRESS
BODICE FRONT
Cut 2

Attach ties ✕

¼-inch seam allowance included

Crocheted Doll

Shown on page 68.

Finished height of doll is 20 inches.

MATERIALS
J. & P. Coats Knit-Cro-Sheen
   crochet thread (225-yard ball):
   3 balls of No. 61 ecru
Size 7 steel crochet hook
Size C aluminum crochet hook
Polyester fiberfill
Ecru sewing thread
⅔ yard of lightweight floral
   fabric for dress and pantaloons
Scrap of striped fabric for apron
1 yard of ½-inch-wide white satin
   ribbon for the apron tie
1 yard of ¼-inch-wide pink satin
   ribbon for the collar bow
Three small white buttons
Size 78mm doll shoes
Size 12-13 curly doll wig
1¼ yds of ¼-inch-wide elastic
Tracing paper

Gauge: 9 dc = 1 inch, 4 rows = 1 inch.
Abbreviations: See page 72.

Stitches used: Chain, slip stitch, single crochet, half double crochet, double crochet, plus the following stitches:

Post st dc: Yo, put hook from front under post of next dc 2 rows down, pull up lp and complete dc.

Dc dec: Holding back on hook last lp of each dc, make dc in each of next 2 sts, yo and draw through rem 3 lps on hook.

INSTRUCTIONS
LEG: Starting at bottom of foot with ecru crochet thread and Size 7 hook, ch 21.

Rnd 1: Make 2 dc in fourth ch from hook, dc in next 16 ch; 5 dc in last ch. Working along opposite side of ch, make 16 more dc across; make 2 dc in same ch as first 2 dc; join with sl st in top of beg ch-3.

Rnd 2: Ch 3, dc in same place as sl st; (2 dc in next dc) twice, dc in 16 dc; (2 dc in next dc) 5 times, dc in 16 dc, 2 dc in each of last 2 dc; join to top of beg ch-3—52 sts, counting beg ch-3.

Rnd 3 (upper sock): Sl st in next dc, ch 3, dc in each st around; join—52 sts.

Rnds 4 and *5:* Ch 3, dc in same place as sl st, dc in next 23 dc; (dc dec over next 2 sts) twice, dc in 23 dc, 2 dc in last dc; join—52 sts.

Rnd 6: Ch 3, dc in same place as sl st, dc in 21 dc; (dc dec over next 2 sts) 4 times, dc in 21 dc, 2 dc in last dc; join—50 sts.

Rnd 7: Ch 3, dc in next 20 dc; (dc dec over next 2 dc) 4 times, dc in last 21 dc; join—46 dc.

Rnd 8: Ch 3, dc dec over next 2 sts, dc in next 16 dc; (dc dec over next 2 sts) 4 times, dc in next 17 dc, dc dec over last 2 sts; join—40 sts.

Rnds 9–12: Ch 3, dc each dc around; join—40 sts.

Rnd 13 (cuff): Ch 1, sc in same place as joining; * work post st dc, sc in next dc; rep from * around; join. *Note:* When making post st, the st above it on last row remains unworked.

Rnd 14: Ch 1, sc in same place as joining, sc in each sc and post st dc around; join—40 sts.

Rnd 15: Ch 1, sc in same place as joining, * post st dc around post st 2 rows down, sc in next sc; rep from * around; join—40 sts.

Rnds 16 and *17:* Rep rnds 14 and 15.

Rnd 18 (leg): Ch 3, dc in each sc and post st dc around, join.

Rnds 19–44: Ch 3, dc in each dc around, join—40 sts; fasten off at end of Rnd 44—27 ecru rows.

Make other leg in the same way.

BODY: Starting at the lower edge with ecru crochet thread, ch 80; join with sl st to form ring.

Rnd 1: Ch 3—to count as first dc; make dc in rem 79 ch; join—80 sts.

Rnds 2–4: Ch 3, dc in each dc around; join—80 sts.

First set of short rows for seat shaping: Sl st in next dc, sc in next 6 dc, hdc in dc, dc in next 22 dc, hdc in dc, sc in 6 dc, sl st in next 2 dc, turn. (Leave rem 40 sts on row unworked.) Sk first sl st, sc in next sl st, sc in 5 sc, hdc in last sc, dc in next 24 sts, hdc in first sc, sc in next 6 sts, sl st in place where rnd starts; turn.

Rnd 5: Ch 3, work 39 dc across seat shaping section, dc in rem 40 dc; join—80 sts.

Second set of short rows: Work same as first set.

Rnd 6: Rep Rnd 5.

Rnds 7–10: Rep rnds 2–4.

Rnd 11 (start waist): Ch 2, dc in next 37 dc; (dc dec over next 2 sts) twice, dc in next 36 dc, dc dec over last 2 dc; sk beg ch-2; join with sl st in first dc—76 sts.

Rnd 12: Ch 2, dc in next 35 dc; (dc dec over next 2 dc) twice, dc in next 34 dc, dc dec over last 2 dc; join like Rnd 11—72 sts.

Rnd 13: Sl st in next dc, ch 3, dc in all other sts around; join.

Rnd 14: Sl st in next dc, ch 3, dc in same st as join, (2 dc in next dc) twice, dc in next 34 dc; 2 dc in last st; join—76 sts.

Rnds 15–20: Rep rnds 13 and 14, increasing 4 sts each even numbered row by having 2 more dc bet inc sections each side—88 sts at end of Rnd 20.

Rnds 21–25: Ch 3, dc in each dc around; join—88 sts; fasten off at end of Rnd 25.

Shoulder seams: Turn the body section wrong side out. Fold in half so seat fullness is in center of back section. There should be 44 sts each side along top edge. Mark center 24 sts with safety pins or colored thread markers. Use double strand of ecru sewing thread to hand-stitch through both layers of outer 10 sts on each side for shoulders. Center 24 sts of both back and front remain unworked for neck.

Rnd 26 (neck): Turn body section right side out. Sk first 19 unworked dc of neck *back*, attach ecru crochet thread with sl st in next dc. Ch 3, make dc in next 4 dc, continue around with dc in 24 sts of neck front and 19 sts rem on back; join—48 sts.

Rnd 27: Ch 3, dc in next 3 dc, dc dec over next 2 sts (side of neck); dc in next 22 dc, dc dec over next 2 sts, dc in last 18 dc; join.

Rnd 28 (start head): Ch 3, dc in same place as joining, 2 dc in each dc around; join—92 sts.

Rnds 29 and *30:* Ch 3, dc in each dc around; join—92 sts.

Rnd 31: Ch 3, dc in same place as joining; (dc in next 22 dc, 2 dc in next dc) 3 times, dc in last 22 dc; join—96 sts.

Rnds 32–36: Ch 3, dc in each dc around; join—96 sts.

Rnd 37: Ch 3; (dc dec over next 2 dc, dc in next 4 dc) around; end with dc in last 3 dc; join—80 sts.

Rnd 38: Ch 3, dc in each dc around; join—80 sts.

Rnd 39: Ch 3, (dc dec over next 2 dc, dc in next 3 dc) around; end with dc in last 2 dc; join—64 sts.

Rnd 40: Rep Rnd 38—64 sts.

Rnd 41: Ch 3, (dc dec over next 2 dc, dc in next 2 dc) around, end with dc in last dc; join—48 sts.

Rnd 42: Ch 3, (dc dec over next 2 dc, dc in next dc) around; end with dc dec over last 2 dc; join—32 sts.

Rnd 43: Ch 3, dc in first dc; (dc dec over next 2 dc) 15 times, sl st in top of first dc—16 sts.

Rnd 44: Rep Rnd 43, having 7 dc dec after first dc; join; fasten off, leaving a 10-inch length of thread. Weave end through tops of sts on this row, draw up and tie off securely.

RIGHT ARM: Starting at tip of hand with ecru crochet thread, ch 5, join with sl st to form ring.

Rnd 1: Ch 3, 9 dc in ring; join—10 sts.

Rnd 2: Ch 3, dc in same place as joining; (dc in next dc, 2 dc in next dc) around, end with dc in last dc; join—15 sts.

Rnd 3: Ch 3, dc in same place as joining; (dc in each of next 2 dc, 2 dc in next dc) around, dc in last 2 dc; join—20 sts.

Rnd 4 (start thumb): Ch 3, (4 dc in next dc) twice, dc in rem 17 dc around; join.

Rnd 5: Ch 3, (dc dec over next 2 dc) 4 times, dc in rem 17 dc around; join.

Rnd 6: Ch 3, (dc dec over next 2 dc) twice, dc in rem 17 dc; join.

Rnd 7 (wrist): Ch 3, dc in each dc around; join—20 sts.

Rnd 8 (start arm): Ch 3, dc in same place as joining; (dc in each of next 3 dc, 2 dc in next dc) around, dc in last 3 dc; join—25 sts.

Rnd 9: Ch 3, dc in same place as joining; (dc in each of next 4 dc, 2 dc in next dc) around, dc in last 4 dc; join—30 sts.

Rnds 10–31: Ch 3, dc in each dc around; join—30 sts; fasten off at end of Rnd 31.

LEFT ARM: Rep rnds 1-3 of Right Arm.

Rnd 4: Ch 3, dc in next 16 dc; (4 dc in next dc) twice, dc in last dc; join.

Rnd 5: Ch 3, dc in next 16 dc; (dc dec over next 2 dc) 4 times, dc in last dc; join.

Rnd 6: Ch 3, dc in next 16 dc; (dc dec over next 2 dc) twice, dc in last dc; join.

Rnd 7–31: Rep rnds 7–31 of Right Arm.

ASSEMBLY: Stuff the body firmly. Cut a 24-inch length of crochet thread and fold it in half. Starting at back of neck, weave double thread through dc of Rnd 27. Pull knot securely, leaving neck about 6½ inches around. Pull thread ends to inside of doll body.

Run another thread from back through Rnd 13 in same manner, pulling up waist to about 8 inches. Use a double strand of sewing thread to whipstitch lower edges of body together.

Stuff lower part of each leg up to Rnd 28. Fold leg so toe of shoe is at center front. With double strand of sewing thread, make running st across top of Rnd 28 (between 11th and 12th crochet rows) for knee joint. Draw up stitching slightly, fasten off.

Stuff upper legs; whipstitch top edges closed. Sew legs to lower edge of body along seam line.

Stuff hand and arm firmly. Fold top of arm flat and whipstitch edges together. Gather edge slightly and sew onto shoulder at right angle to shoulder seam. Take care that thumb of each arm is pointing toward front of body.

CLOTHING: Use ¼-inch seams on all stitching. Full-size clothing patterns are on pages 78 and 79.

Transfer patterns to tracing paper; cut out. From floral fabric, cut two each of pantaloons, collar, and bodice back; cut one bodice front on fold. Cut 11x30-inch rectangle for skirt.

From striped fabric, cut one 9½x14-inch apron rectangle.

PANTALOONS: Hem bottom edge of legs. Stitch a 5-inch piece of elastic on wrong side ½ inch above each hemmed edge. Stitch one center seam (for front). Fold over ¾ inch at top for elastic casing, turn under raw edge, and

stitch down. Run an 8-inch piece of elastic through the casing, tack down at each end. Stitch remaining center seam (for back) and leg seam, catching elastic in seams.

DRESS: Stitch shoulder and down top of sleeves between X markings on bodice/sleeve pattern; press seams open.

Make two ¼-inch tucks on each side of the center of the bodice front. Machine-topstitch tucks flat.

Turn neck edge inside ¼ inch and stitch. Hem bottom edges of sleeves. Sew a 4-inch piece of elastic on wrong side of each sleeve ½ inch above hemmed edge. Stretch elastic as you sew to create full gathering. Sew underarm seams of bodice/sleeve.

Gather one 30-inch side of skirt fabric to fit dress bodice. With right sides together, stitch bodice to skirt. Starting at bottom of skirt, stitch center back seam for 6 inches, leaving the remainder of the seam open. Sew 2-inch-wide hem at bottom of skirt. Turn both edges of bodice back and opening of skirt to the inside and topstitch. Sew one snap closure at the neckline and one at the waist of the bodice back. Sew three small white buttons to center front of dress. Put dress on doll.

COLLAR: With right sides facing, sew collar pieces together. Leave a 1-inch opening along the back for turning. Turn collar right side out; topstitch around collar.

Attach one 12-inch length of pink ribbon to each side of the collar. Tie at doll's neck.

APRON: Hem one long and two short sides of striped apron fabric rectangle. Turn second long edge of fabric under 1 inch (this is the top edge). Gather the top edge to measure 6½ inches. Center and topstitch ½-inch white ribbon over top of stitching to make waistband. Tie at doll's waist.

SHOES AND WIG: Purchase doll shoes and wig from your local doll supply shop or send inquiries to Jo's Dolls, 111 Army Post Rd., Des Moines, IA 50315.

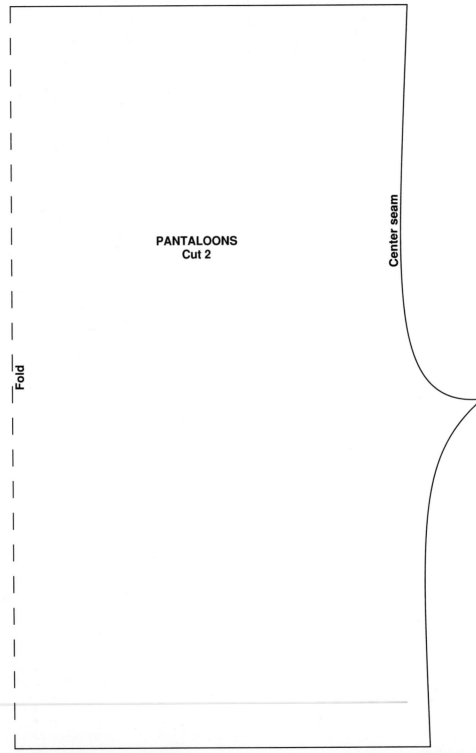

PANTALOONS
Cut 2

Fold

Center seam

CROCHETED DOLL CLOTHING
¼-inch seam allowance included

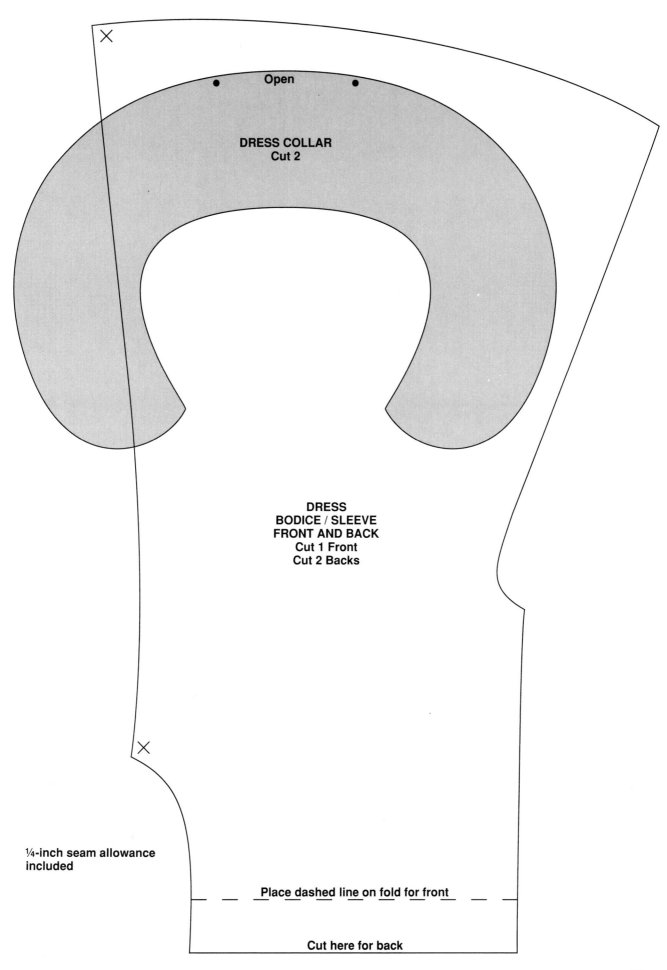

Open

DRESS COLLAR
Cut 2

DRESS
BODICE / SLEEVE
FRONT AND BACK
Cut 1 Front
Cut 2 Backs

¼-inch seam allowance
included

Place dashed line on fold for front

Cut here for back

ACKNOWLEDGMENTS

We would like to extend our special thanks to the following designers who contributed projects to this book.

Pam Dyer—42–43

Pam Fordyce—66–67

Phoebe Greathouse—26–27, 28–29

JoAnn Gummere—8–9

Cindy Hurlbut—cover, 4–5

Gayle Kinkead—68

Jan Lewis—30–31

Lois Liden—48–49, 50–51

Beth MacDonald—69

Beverly Rivers—6–7

Margaret Sindelar—20–21

Judy Veeder—52–53

We are pleased to acknowledge the photographers whose talents and technical skills contributed much to this book.

William Hopkins, Jr.—cover, 4–5, 26–31, 48–53, 66–67

Perry Struse—6–9, 20–21, 42–43, 68–69

For their cooperation and courtesy, we extend a special thanks to the following sources for providing materials for projects and props for photography.

All Cooped Up Designs
560 S. State, No. B1
Orem, UT 84058
   for doll hair on pages 6, 7, and 20

Beyond the Garden Gate
1998 N.W. 92nd Court, Suite A
Des Moines, IA 50325
   for nosegay and cake top on pages 20–21

Brunswick Yarns
Pickens, SC 29671
   for doll yarn on page 68

Coats & Clark, Inc.
Dept. C.S.
P.O. Box 1010
Toccoa, GA 30577
   for doll thread on page 69

The DMC Corporation
P.O. Box 500
Port Kearny, Building 10
South Kearny, NJ 07032-0500
   for embroidery floss

Donna's Dolls & Country Collection
234 5th Street
West Des Moines, IA 50265
   for doll props and accessories

Nancy Hopkins
   for dollhouse on pages 52–53

Jo's Dolls-N-Fine Porcelain
111 Army Post Road
Des Moines, IA 50315
   for doll wig on page 69, hat and roses on page 7, and shoes on pages 6, 7, and 69

Tom Keller
   for bicycle on page 30